HEARTPRINTS

Leslie ~
God bless your
heartprints!
Sandra P. Aldrich
Ece. 4:9-10

Celebrating the Power
of a Simple Touch

HeartPrints

Sandra Picklesimer Aldrich

Bobbie Valentine

WaterBrook
PRESS

HEARTPRINTS
PUBLISHED BY WATERBROOK PRESS
2375 Telstar Drive, Suite 160
Colorado Springs, Colorado 80920
A division of Random House, Inc.

All Scripture quotations are taken from the *Holy Bible, New International Version®*. NIV® Copyright © 1973, 1978, 1984 by International Bible Society. Used by permission of Zondervan Publishing House. All rights reserved.

Special thanks to Ruth Harms Calkin for permission to reprint her poem "HeartPrints" from *Lord, Could You Hurry a Little?* Copyright © 1983. Used by permission. All rights reserved.

Details in some anecdotes and stories have been changed to protect the identities of the persons involved.

ISBN 1-57856-428-X

Published in association with the literary agency of
Alive Communications, Inc., 7680 Goddard Street
Suite 200, Colorado Springs, CO 80920

Printed in the United States of America

2001

10 9 8 7 6 5 4 3 2

Contents

Acknowledgments

What an adventure writing this book has been. First, our special thanks to Greg Johnson of Alive Communications, Inc., for introducing us to WaterBrook Press. The privilege of working with Rebecca Price, vice president of marketing, Traci Mullins, editor, and Laura Barker, managing editor, has left additional "heartprints" upon our lives. We're also grateful to Jan Nations for her diligence in transcribing hours of the interview tapes.

The lovely poem "Heartprints," from which the title of the book comes, was written by Ruth Harms Calkin and has appeared in her book *Lord, Could You Hurry a Little?* We'd like to thank her for distilling into these few lines the quiet but awesome impact our actions can have each day. Further, we appreciate her graciousness in granting permission for us to use her poem in this book. To Ruth Harms Calkin, we offer our hearty appreciation for *her* heartprints.

The lion's share of our gratitude goes to the women who graciously shared their real-life stories and granted us permission to use them in *HeartPrints* with only an occasional name change. Without their generosity, this book would have remained a dream. It is our hope that other women not only will enjoy reading these true stories but will find renewed purpose as they realize the incredible difference they too can make in the lives of others.

Heartprints

Whatever our hands touch—
We leave fingerprints!
On walls, on furniture,
On doorknobs, dishes, books,
As we touch we leave our identity.

O God, wherever I go today,
Help me to leave heartprints!
Heartprints of compassion,
Of understanding and love.
Heartprints of kindness
And genuine concern.

May my heart touch a lonely neighbor,
Or a runaway daughter,
Or an anxious mother,
Or, perhaps, a dear friend!

Lord, send me out today
To leave heartprints.
And if someone should say,
"I felt your touch,"
May that one sense YOUR LOVE
Touching through ME.

— Ruth Harms Calkin

Introduction

To Make a Difference

Lisa smiled at the four-month-old baby in her arms as he enjoyed a morning bottle. The church nursery was uncharacteristically quiet this Sunday. Normally, four or five of the infants would be crying as the attendants wound the musical swings, gave bottles, and changed diapers.

But now Lisa and Marilee actually had a moment to catch up as they rocked babies. Marilee, a likeable, talkative woman, told Lisa, "I was at the women's prison again Thursday. That's such a big place, almost eight hundred inmates now. It breaks your heart to go there. A new woman who calls herself 'Cat' just sits there staring at me. She doesn't follow along in the text or join the discussions. I asked the chaplain about her, but he didn't have much to say other than she's had a rough life, like most of the others in there. So I'm asking the Lord to use me to make a difference in her life."

What a wonderful ministry, Lisa thought as she snuggled the baby in her arms. *But I could never go to a prison and teach the Bible. I just don't have special gifts like Marilee does.*

1

What Lisa doesn't realize is that she is already doing something special by lovingly caring for the babies in the nursery two Sundays a month. The young mothers can enjoy the worship service and get the spiritual encouragement they need since they know their children are safe. Several of them even find themselves calmed by Lisa's gentleness toward their children and try to incorporate that attitude into their own responses at home. If they were to try to express that to Lisa, however, she undoubtedly would brush aside their comments, not realizing what an important role she is playing in their lives.

To make a difference is our heart's basic cry, but it may take effort on our part to see that we do have extraordinary worth—not only to God but to those around us. We are prone to think that only a dramatic public act of service is important. However, it is more often than not the quiet kindnesses that leave their marks on hearts and lives. In these pages you will read about some of the extraordinary "heartprints" ordinary women have gently stamped upon others, usually without realizing their impact.

For instance, Jean, an executive in a large Christian organization, has made two moves within the past five years, but none of her town-house neighbors have welcomed her. She confesses that since she's not an outgoing person, she didn't knock on their doors either. So every night, like countless other people, she pulled into her parking spot, got her mail, and silently entered her home—all without the greeting of another person.

This continued until Jean decided to watch for other newcomers to the complex. When a single mother and her two young children moved into the next building, Jean showed up at her door the following Saturday morning with a bright smile, a plate of cookies—and her phone number in case the woman ever needed her help. What an impact that simple, friendly gesture had on the recent divorcée who felt as though she had been abandoned not only by her husband but by the world.

Trish understands abandonment. Often left alone during childhood, she gleaned her concept of femininity from the after-school "soaps." When a suicide attempt in college sent her to counseling, she had to face her longing for motherly direction. "When my counselor suggested I find someone to take my mother's place emotionally," she says, "my first thought was *How do I do that?! Go up to someone in the grocery store and say, 'Will you be my mother?'* My counselor finally suggested I move in with his family for a week so I could see firsthand how his wife mothered their children.

"That first night I listened to her going to the

children's rooms at bedtime to pray with them and then to tuck them in. When she came into my room to say good night, she actually sat on the bed and offered to pray with me too. My prayer was pretty short because I was so choked up—nobody had ever done that with me before—but when she tucked the blanket around me and bent down to kiss my forehead, I absolutely lost it. She did more for me in that one evening than all of her husband's counseling ever could."

None of these stories are parting-of-the-Red-Sea scenarios. Rather they tell about one woman simply reaching out to another—through a plate of cookies, a friendly smile, a kiss on the forehead, a prayer, a servant's heart. Every day women make a profound difference in others' lives through simple acts of sharing God's love. Our most artless action can become a profound, life-changing heartprint that will not only touch one woman's life but ripple out to others. And we don't know how far that influence will go—perhaps even from generation to generation, as the women we influence then touch the lives of those around them.

If you were to ask the average woman what she could do to influence others, she probably would be astounded by the question and might even say, "Oh, I'm not talented. I can't do anything special." Often these are the women who sit in church week after week and feel that since they don't have a public ministry, they couldn't possibly make a difference. They think, *I can't get up in front of people. I can't teach. I'm so busy just being a mother I don't have time to do anything for God. I don't know enough Scripture. God could never use me. I'm not a missionary.*

But these same women—women just like you— already are being used by God every day! As you absorb the Word and spend time with God in prayer, you are empowered to be a friend, to care, to open your heart and home, to put an arm around weary shoulders. To leave heartprints wherever you go.

In the following pages, you'll read true stories about women who, often without being aware of it, deeply impacted others through their simple lives and deeds. May you come to recognize the incredible impact you too are having on those around you as you walk across their lives in love.

ENCOURAGEMENT

Therefore encourage one another and build each
other up, just as in fact you are doing.

1 THESSALONIANS 5:11

Perfume and incense bring joy to the heart,
    and the pleasantness of one's friend
        springs from his earnest counsel.
Do not forsake your friend and the friend of
        your father,
    and do not go to your brother's house when
        disaster strikes you—
    better a neighbor nearby than a brother far away.

PROVERBS 27:9-10

Two are better than one,
    because they have a good return for their work:
If one falls down,
    his friend can help him up.
But pity the man who falls
    and has no one to help him up!

ECCLESIASTES 4:9-10

The Ministry of Refreshment

Have you noticed that often it is the timing of a thoughtful gesture, rather than its scope, that makes the difference?...

For a lonesome serviceman or woman that refreshing lift could be a timely letter or a card. For a frazzled couple with young children, it could be an offer to baby-sit so they can go out for an evening or a weekend get-away. For a discouraged Christian worker it could be a weekend at a conference or a retreat. For an elderly person or shut-in a card, a call, or a visit could be the highlight of the week. For a student feeling pressured and homesick, it might be an offer to go out to lunch, or to help study for an exam. For a frustrated Sunday school director who can't seem to find anyone who will help, it could be an offer to fill in wherever you're needed most.

The ministry of refreshment involves genuine concern, willingness to take risks, and persistence in service. It requires being alert to the needs of others and seeking to provide relief from the pressures that burden them. . . .

The Lord has promised that those who hope in Him shall gain new strength and be renewed (Is. 40:29-31). He may use a supernatural means to fulfill this promise. Is it possible, though, that He might want to use a human instrument . . . ? Might He want to use . . . you?[1]

—STEPHEN HOPPER

Chapter One

The Power of a Hug

Dawn kept blinking as she sorted through the files on her desk. *Come on, concentrate,* she demanded of herself. *This is your first day here, and you need this job, remember?*

As though she could forget. She was still reeling from the news her policeman husband had given her several weeks earlier. It was the day after Thanksgiving when he told Dawn he had fallen in love with his female partner. He was sorry to hurt her, he said, but he thought it was better to be up-front about it rather than sneak around. This way, he said, she wouldn't have to guess. Sorry to mess up her Christmas holidays, but he thought he should give her a heads-up so she could get on with her life.

Dawn looked up a tracking number, wishing she could find answers to her own questions and challenges as easily. She still wasn't sure she would *survive,* let alone "get on" with life. The holidays had been awful. How do you explain a father's absence at Christmas to three young children? How was she going to stay sane with all she had to juggle? She couldn't do this. That's all there was to it. Tears threatened to spill onto her cheeks.

Where's that tissue? Come on, Dawn, get with it. Tears aren't helping. Nobody cares anyway.

As she turned toward her computer to input the list of upcoming projects, a cheery voice called from the doorway, "Hi! May I bother you for a moment? I need some information."

Dawn looked up to see a woman whose smile faded as soon as she saw Dawn's face. She quickly stepped into the young woman's office.

"It looks like you could use a hug!" she said as she held out her arms.

A hug was exactly what Dawn needed, and without hesitation she stood up to lean against the woman's ample shoulders.

Suddenly the woman was praying in Dawn's ear: "Lord, you know all the details that caused these tears, so I ask that you wipe them away by letting her know you haven't forgotten her. Help her with her challenges, Lord, and throughout this day—and the days ahead—give her a squeeze just as tangible as this one. Let her feel your presence. May she know you are with her."

Only at her *amen* did the woman release Dawn from the embrace. Then she pulled a folded tissue from her jacket pocket and handed it to Dawn, who blew her nose.

The woman introduced herself as Karen,* then said, "Now, I'm going to pray for you as often as the Lord brings you to mind, so feel free to call my extension anytime you need a quick prayer."

Dawn nodded her thanks, then managed to say, "You don't know how much I needed your encouragement just now."

Karen smiled. "Well, the Lord knew. Hang on to that, and don't let any 'turkeys' win!"

Dawn smiled for the first time in months as Karen emphasized the word "turkeys." Dawn liked this woman.

Throughout that year Karen always seemed to stop by just when Dawn needed a motherly hug and a prayer. With each hug came encouragement to be the best person she could be. After those times, Dawn always had the sensation that she had been set back on her feet. Oh, her unwanted divorce still went through, and she's still juggling all the responsibilities of being a single mother of three active children. Today, however, she knows that she has enormous value in the eyes of God. After all, he cared enough to send her an angel bearing hugs!

———————

*Not her real name

To Ponder:

Karen was just an ordinary woman who put an arm around someone in need and said an encouraging word. In that moment she became "God with skin on" for a young, hurting mother.

Can you hug someone who is in despair? If God lets you glimpse the hurt in someone else, you can be his arms encircling her and affirming God's love for her.

Give Someone a Hug Today

It's wondrous what a hug can do.
A hug can cheer you when you're blue.
A hug can say, "I love you so,"
Or "I sure hate to see you go."

A hug is "Welcome back again!"
And, "Great to see you, where've you been?"
A hug can soothe a small child's pain,
And brings a rainbow after rain.

The hug. There's no doubt about it.
We scarcely could survive without it.
A hug delights and warms and charms.
It must be why God gave us arms.

Hugs are great for fathers and mothers,
Sweet for sisters, swell for brothers.
And chances are your favorite aunts
Love them more than potted plants.

Kittens crave them, puppies love them,
Heads of state are not above them.
A hug can break the language barrier,
Make your travel so much merrier.

No need to fret about your store of them.
The more you give, the more there's of them.
So stretch those arms without delay
And give someone a hug today.[2]

—AUTHOR UNKNOWN

14

Chapter Two

Dear Virginia

Linda Williams trudged through the December snow after her last class of the day. Even though the post office had sent the yellow slip saying she had a certified letter waiting, she was in no hurry. She wouldn't hurry until March, when she expected to hear from the University of Colorado whether she had been accepted into their medical school. If today's letter was from them, it was probably a standard form letter regretting to inform her that her age did not make her a good candidate for medical school. *Am I too old at twenty-seven?* Linda wondered.

Well, she'd get their rejection and then get on with life. She would finish this third year of the pre-med program and then go back to nursing. Oh, but she would dread telling Virginia Trevitt.

Dear Virginia. Just remembering the widow's kind face, framed by gray hair, made Linda smile. They'd met through the international educational corporation Up With People on one of its world tours. Linda had been the group's nurse, and Virginia coordinated the education program granting the students college credit for their participation. Virginia was one of the few people Linda was comfortable telling about her background, including her parents' ugly divorce that had resulted in her years in foster care. Further, Virginia had understood the trauma of her working as a public health nurse during the Zenia, Ohio, tornado that had killed almost three dozen people, many of whom were her patients. Linda had come up out of a basement that day to find herself looking directly into the murky sky and standing in rubble where modest, well-kept homes had been only moments before.

The two women chatted over tea as Virginia suddenly asked, "What do you think God wants you to do with your life?"

Without thinking, Linda blurted, "Be a doctor."

Then she fell silent, astonished at what had tumbled out of her mouth. *Where did that come from?* she wondered.

She remembered the elementary school paper she had written on herbs and healing. And the Christmas she had asked for a Ben Casey doctor's kit. For her high school senior term paper, she had researched the first heart transplant. But her sad home life and years in foster care had convinced her that even with good grades, she couldn't become a doctor. After graduation she had enrolled in a nursing program instead.

Virginia's voice had interrupted Linda's musings. "So, why haven't you become a doctor?" she asked.

Linda stammered, "I want a family."

Virginia looked thoughtful. "I thought you said you were a Christian."

"I am."

"Well, then, your life is not your own," Virginia said gently. "You can't use the label of 'Christian' if your life is controlled by what you want."

"But you know my background. I can't do something like that," Linda cried.

Virginia frowned. "And you can't use the label of 'Christian' if your life is controlled by fear."

Virginia continued, "I'm going to pray about this every day for the next six months, and I want you to pray too. You can finish your time with us and then go home and pick up where you left off, or you can be part of what God wants to do in your life."

Linda tried to argue. "But I don't have any money," she said, pleading her case. "I don't have family to help me. And I don't know any doctors personally."

Virginia sipped her tea, then said, "If God wants you to be a doctor, *he* will provide. Let's pray about it right now."

And they did. Shortly after that visit, Linda was assigned to Venezuela with Up With People. During one rare afternoon off, she took a long walk and found herself standing in front of the Venezuelan International Library. Feeling drawn inside, she asked for the medical section, where she found a volume listing requirements and addresses of numerous undergraduate schools for pre-med studies.

As she dug in her purse for a pen and paper, she whispered, "Okay, Virginia, you said to let God pitch. So I will at least be brave enough to step to the plate."

To her great amazement, that afternoon so long ago produced acceptance into a pre-med program.

Now in her third year of pre-med studies, Linda climbed the granite steps of the post office. Taking a deep breath, she prayed inwardly, *God, was this dream of you? I'm a person of little faith, so please confirm my path—one way or another.*

Pulling on the heavy doors, Linda took her place in the long line of people waiting to mail Christmas packages. When it was finally her turn, the man at the counter handed her a manilla envelope. Yes, it was from the University of Colorado's Health Sciences Center all right. *Well, at least I tried,* she thought.

Sighing, she moved down the counter, out of the way, and slowly loosened the envelope flap. The letter on top of numerous forms began, "Dear Miss Williams: We are pleased to invite you to join our class of . . ."

What?! Linda reread the first sentence. *We are pleased to invite you . . .* She paused, then read it again. *Wait! This means they've accepted me!*

Suddenly she let out a joyful whoop. As people in line turned to look at her, she grabbed the nearest woman in a great bear hug.

"I've been accepted!" she shouted. "The University of Colorado medical school said yes! I'm going to be a doctor."

Everyone smiled, and several people applauded.

Linda couldn't wait to get back to her apartment to call Virginia. She knew that during the next four years tough times undoubtedly were ahead—financial worries, endless student loans, long hours—but if the Lord had opened this impossible door, he'd open others, just as Virginia had said.

Virginia, of course, was delighted by Linda's news and became a faithful correspondent, sending at least a postcard every other day for years. Her letters were encouraging and filled with wisdom. Often it seemed as though God himself was writing through her to redirect Linda's thinking just when she needed it most: "God has given you a calling, so he will give you the strength" or "Yes, you are capable. God already has given you what you need. I know the work is hard, but remember that 'To whom much is given, much is required.'"

At the end of Linda's first year of medical school, Virginia invited her to spend a few days with her. Waiting for her on the bed was a brightly wrapped package containing four china cups and saucers. The accompanying note said, "As you drink your tea, remember the evening you found your dream."

Even after Virginia's retirement from Up With

People and her return to her home state of California, she would invite Linda to visit once a year for the few days the young woman could spare from her studies. During that time Virginia pampered Linda as lovingly as any mother has ever pampered a daughter, even insisting upon serving her breakfast in bed.

Daily they would walk the beach. One night they took raspberry sundaes along as they listened to waves rolling against the sand in the dark. That evening Virginia shared some of the amazing things she had learned in her almost seventy years, including story after story of God's provision.

Taking a bite of her sundae, Virginia said, "When you've run out of ideas and plans, Linda, that's when God works best. He can't do for us if we're too busy doing for ourselves. So don't worry when frustrating times come—and they will come with irritating frequency—just remember that the Lord put this dream in your heart, so he'll see you through. God is limitless. All of us were put here to make a difference, and you are part of what God is doing on this earth."

In that moment Linda felt as though she could do anything.

Virginia's encouragement continued for four years.

On graduation day Linda joyfully accepted her diploma, then clutched the precious document to her chest. As she returned to her seat, she smiled toward the section where she knew Virginia sat, beaming with pride. But the older woman wasn't the least bit surprised by Linda's achievement. She'd always known the dream would come true. And why not? After all, God was the one who placed it in Linda's heart. It just needed Virginia's prodding to uncover it.

———————

To Ponder:

Virginia allowed God to use her to encourage younger people who came across her path. Today Linda Williams is a prominent family practice physician who not only deals with the health issues in her patients' lives but passes on the spiritual encouragement that Virginia gave to her.

Do you know a young person who needs some encouragement? Ask God to give you the insight to encourage the people who cross your path.

Pleasant Words

Pleasant words are a honeycomb,
　　sweet to the soul and healing to the bones.

—PROVERBS 16:24

I'm sure if you thought a little you could think of someone who did this for you. Someone who called and just said the right thing on a really bad day. . . Someone who reminded you that you're a terrific mother, a great wife, or a wonderful friend. Pleasant words really are sweet to the soul and healing to the bones. Don't fail to give some away![3]

—VICKIE KRAFT

Chapter Three

Breakfast Riddles

Sandra learned to look for each day's joys the morning she found another streak of gray in her hair. And she learned it all from someone who at first glance didn't have anything to offer other than an empty seat in her breakfast booth.

Early that Friday morning, Sandra had peered into the mirror as she brushed her hair. The wing of gray at her right temple had widened almost overnight. She tossed the brush onto the bathroom counter. It was definitely a day for breakfast at her favorite coffee shop.

The Coffee Shop in the middle of Mount Kisco, New York, was one of those narrow, 1950s style diners too busy serving breakfast to early morning workers to bother with the latest tile colors or soda machines. The five booths and dozen counter stools had been witness to almost forty years of World Series arguments, weather complaints, and social changes. Through it all, the grill had sizzled with over-easy eggs and plump hamburgers.

The counter stools were always occupied first, so Sandra and her children, Jay and Holly, usually had no trouble getting a booth. That morning, however, even the booths were filled. The three of them stood by the door for a moment, surrounded by the combined smell of bacon grease, grilled bagels, and strong coffee, wondering if anyone was about to leave.

Suddenly an ancient woman in the back booth waved for them to join her. After their move from Michigan, the trio had quickly learned that New Yorkers are used to sharing their space, so they weren't surprised by the invitation. They smiled their thanks and moved to the offered seats. Holly slid into the booth next to the old woman, while Sandra and Jay sat down across from them.

Sandra thanked the woman for her kindness, then introduced herself and both young teens. The woman smiled and nodded but merely pointed to her ear and shook her head. *Oh, dear. She's deaf,* Sandra thought.

The three sat in uncomfortable silence while the woman continued with her breakfast. Her red, arthritic hands cut the poached egg on toast as Sandra stared at her own hands, knowing that someday they would be gnarled like hers. *Wasn't it enough that I found the new streak of gray this morning?* Sandra thought. *Did I have to get this second reminder of my own mortality too?* She looked at Jay and Holly and

flashed her standard "It's okay" smile while t̶
woman's hands continued to move in her side visio̶

Sandra forced her thoughts to other details of u̶u̶
woman's person. The collar of her flowered, navy blue
dress peeked over the top of her tightly buttoned
maroon sweater. Tinted glasses sat on the end of her
nose. Her hair was silver and covered by a bright blue
winter cap.

What color had her hair been? Nondescript
brunette like Sandra's? Or perhaps chestnut, its red
highlights tossing bits of sunlight toward an admiring
beau? Had her swollen hands once gently held babies
who grew up and left for exotic places, remembering
her only at Christmas and Mother's Day, if then? Had
those same hands tenderly sponged the feverish forehead of an ill husband who died, despite her care,
leaving her to grow old alone?

At last the woman put her knife and fork across
the plate, drank the last of her heavily creamed coffee,
and then leaned toward Holly. "Why do you go to bed
at night?" she asked.

Because the three of them wrongly had assumed
the woman was probably mute as well as deaf, her
question momentarily startled them. Finally Holly
shrugged and answered, "Because I'm tired?"

The woman, who had watched Holly's lips closely,
leaned forward, the sparkle in her eyes suddenly

25

apparent. "Because the bed won't come to you!" she exclaimed.

The three laughed appreciatively then, so she tapped the table surface in front of Jay. "If I put a quarter and a nickel here, and the nickel rolled off, why didn't the quarter?"

Jay and Sandra looked at each other in puzzlement. The woman smiled as she supplied the answer with obvious delight: "Because the quarter has more sense!"

Her unexpected play on words was so comical that they all laughed. Sandra waited for another riddle, but the woman busied herself with gathering her newspaper and purse. Holly stood up to let her out of the booth. The woman smiled at Sandra, patted Holly's shoulder, gripped Jay's hand in farewell, and was off, her head up and her stooped shoulders momentarily straightened for the day ahead.

The booth suddenly seemed empty. Sandra's immediate sense of loss was so evident that Holly asked, "What's wrong, Mom?"

Sandra stared at her for a moment. Yes, what was wrong? Actually, nothing was wrong, but something was indeed gone. That dear, elderly woman had given the three of them a moment of unexpected joy, serendipitous encouragement, and Sandra wanted to relish it a little longer.

In those few moments they'd spent together,

Sandra had seen no self-pity, heard no laments for what had been lost, and received no admonishment that Sandra enjoy these "best days of her life" with her children. The woman had merely invited the three of them to share her private joy and, in doing so, had demonstrated a more noble way to face life's challenges.

Sandra smiled at the memory of those sparkling eyes. And that memory helped her accept the new gray streak in her hair as merely another well-earned milestone. *When I'm her age,* Sandra told herself, *I hope I'm also teaching others to grab today's joy.* For now, Sandra decided, she would rejoice in what she had left instead of lamenting what she had lost. And that was a good lesson to have learned so early in life.

To Ponder:

From outward appearances and actions, the elderly woman had nothing to offer but a seat in a dining booth. But from this unexpected source came a new perspective on life for Sandra. The woman could have quietly finished her meal and left, not reaching out nor revealing her sense of humor. Instead she chose to touch others' lives by focusing on the joy and humor in the moment.

As you focus on everything you have instead of what you may have lost, God can use you. What opportunities do you have to express Christian joy in front of others?

Imperfect Vessels

The exciting truth I want you to grab hold of is this: God can use imperfect vessels like you and me. In fact, he often delights in choosing the most unlikely people to accomplish his purposes in this world. Everyone around you may consider you the least likely job candidate, but fortunately, God works as his own employment recruiter! No matter who you are, if you will yield your life to God, you can become a vessel God can use.[4]

—DONNA PARTOW

PRAYER

Do not be anxious about anything, but in everything, by prayer and petition, with thanksgiving, present your requests to God. And the peace of God, which transcends all understanding, will guard your hearts and your minds in Christ Jesus.

PHILIPPIANS 4:6-7

Cast all your anxiety on him because he cares for you.

1 PETER 5:7

The LORD is good,
    a refuge in times of trouble.
He cares for those who trust in him.

NAHUM 1:7

Chapter Four

A New Beginning

Amber* looked out the window, hoping to see her son's car pull into the drive. *Where was he this time?* she worried. *In jail? In a ditch?*

She paced the kitchen. Sure, Chet* was an adult. And this wasn't the first time he'd gone off drinking and been out all night. But this time he'd been gone for two nights. Something was wrong. Very wrong. She looked at the phone, wishing it would ring, then afraid it might. She had to stop this.

Please, Lord, she thought. Wait, that was it; she needed Brenda* to pray. If anyone knew how to connect with God, it was Brenda. As Amber nervously dialed the phone and then listened to the rings, she thought of Brenda's quiet prayers that had gotten this family through numerous crises, starting with Amber's daughter and five-year-old granddaughter moving in after a nasty divorce and custody battle. Amber remembered how the traumatized child had cried constantly. Surely none of them could have made it

---

* Not their real names

through the adjustment if it hadn't been for Brenda's prayers. And now Amber definitely needed to feel God's presence anew.

When Brenda answered the phone, Amber's fears burst out. "Chet hasn't been home for two nights, and I'm worried sick!" she said. "He's never stayed out this long. He has identification, so surely if he were in jail or injured, someone would call me. But what do I do now?"

Brenda's gentle voice calmed Amber immediately. "The first thing we're going to do is pray," she said, and she began softly, "Father, we thank you that you know where Chet is. And we thank you that you *are* working even if we can't see it . . ."

As Brenda prayed, Amber felt as though peace, like a thick warm blanket, was being gently draped around her shoulders. At Brenda's confident *amen,* Amber felt calm for the first time in two days.

"Now, as soon as we hang up," Brenda said, "I'm going to call my prayer group and ask them to pray too. Then I'm coming over, so put on the teapot. Remember, the Lord is faithful. And until I get there, consider yourself hugged!"

Amber could almost feel the familiar hug right through the phone. As she filled the teakettle, she was grateful to have something to do while she waited for her dear friend. They had met when they and their husbands had served each Sunday morning at their church's Visitor Center. Gradually, as Amber learned to trust Brenda, she confided that her son Chet was an alcoholic. For more than a decade the family had been dealing with the painful effects of the disease, and Amber found it hard to have faith that Chet would ever get well.

As she waited for Brenda's arrival, Amber pulled mugs and spicy tea bags out of the cabinet, amazed at how hopeful she suddenly felt. When the bell rang, she jerked open the door and threw her arms around her friend.

As soon as the two were seated at the kitchen table, steaming mugs cupped in their hands, Brenda asked Amber what she wanted God to do.

"I've been asking him to bring Chet home right now!" Amber answered.

Brenda nodded. "I can certainly understand that," she said. "But God is in control. He knows where Chet is. We can trust the Lord's answer—even when we don't like it. His will always makes the situation right."

Then Brenda started to pray, "Lord, you know where Chet is, and you know what you want to do to get his attention. We trust you, Lord . . ."

Amber, by now, was quietly weeping. When Brenda finished her prayer, she hugged Amber, then wiped away her own tears.

"I'm going to keep praying every day until you

know Chet is safe," Brenda said. "Remember, God is working even when we can't see him."

The next five days were rough indeed because Amber still did not hear from her son. But every morning and evening Brenda called to get a report and to pray with Amber again.

Then on the evening of the fifth day, Amber heard the front door open. She looked up to see Chet walking toward her with outstretched arms.

"Mom, I've been in detox," he said as he hugged her.

Amber looked confused. "What?" she stammered.

He gave her shoulders another squeeze. "Everything is going to be okay," he said. "God and I are going to beat this thing."

Bewildered, Amber backed into a chair as she gestured for details.

"Five days ago I woke up in the park vomiting blood," Chet explained. "I looked up and saw a hospital. I had to pull myself up by clutching the trunk of a nearby tree, but I finally managed to stumble to the emergency room. I checked myself in and went through five days of alcohol withdrawal under medical supervision."

Five days ago? Amber thought. *Why, that was the morning I called Brenda!* While Chet was vomiting blood, Amber and Brenda were presenting him to the heavenly Father.

Amber stood up to joyfully hug her son again. Oh, she knew the problem wasn't licked yet, but she also knew this was a new beginning. What had seemed for so long an impossible problem to solve was suddenly infused with hope. God had taken a young man's desperate plight and was turning it into something good—just as Brenda had said he would.

To Ponder:

In a crisis we all need someone to whom we can turn for strength and courage. Brenda's gentle, confident faith allowed her just to "be there" for Amber, while her loving prayers reminded her friend that we can trust God even when we don't understand his ways. Amber wanted her son home right then, but God knew that Chet had to hit bottom before he would take the first step toward recovery.

Have you ever had a friend who was with you in a crisis and who encouraged you to entrust the situation to God? Can you be that kind of friend to someone else?

God Has a Plan

[God] has given each of us the gift of life with a specific purpose in view. To Him work is a sacrament, even what we consider unimportant, mundane work. . . . For each of us, He does have a plan. What joy to find it and even out of our helplessness, let Him guide us in its fulfillment.[5]

—CATHERINE MARSHALL

Chapter Five

Wounded Warrior

Aimee-Kate* looked out her apartment window into the beautiful California morning, wishing she had the energy to go outside. But why bother? By staying in, she didn't have to fight the choking panic that would sweep over her whenever she ventured beyond her door.

When the attacks first occurred years earlier, she had made an immediate appointment with her doctor. But after running the usual medical tests, he had suggested an appointment with a counselor. Well, she'd since seen counselor after counselor. They all said her agoraphobia was a result of problems rooted in her childhood. But the "diagnosis" didn't provide a solution, and medication was only a temporary measure to treat the symptoms rather than the cause.

Aimee-Kate sighed, then turned away from the window. "Lord, I feel thrown out by the world," she whispered. Settling herself on the sofa, she picked up her Bible and pulled out cards and clippings she'd saved that depicted Jesus with children—children on

---

* Not her real name

his lap, leaning against him. She especially liked the one of the giggling little girl with her arms clasped tightly around the neck of a smiling Jesus. *What would it be like to have been hugged so solidly and wonderfully like that?* she thought.

Aimee-Kate had been the child who was always different. Her painful shyness and numerous fears had especially irritated her mother. With a grimace Aimee-Kate remembered the time her mother smacked her behind with a fly swatter in front of the family. Aimee-Kate had long forgotten the reason for the action, but the shame she'd felt had been worse than the sting on her skin. Now Aimee-Kate thought with dismay, *I'm forty-four years old, and I still want my mother to love me.*

The counselors had said her mother wasn't capable of giving unconditional love and that Aimee-Kate had to accept reality. But Aimee-Kate remembered her mother showing great affection toward a younger sibling. *It was just me,* she thought. *I must have been the type that even a mother couldn't love.*

Aimee-Kate had married too young in order to get away from home. But the familiar rejection came again when her husband left her for another woman. Now here she was—divorced, a single mother of a teen daughter, and feeling totally useless to others. How she longed for a friend who would call or send a note to say, "Hey, I'm praying for you. How are you today?"

Well, that wasn't happening. And she couldn't do anything except ask the Lord to help others who had deep needs. So, with the pictures of Jesus and the children still on her lap, she picked up last Sunday's church bulletin and turned to the back page, where the names of homebound or hospitalized members were listed. Even though few details were given, Aimee-Kate touched her fingertips to each name and whispered her prayers:

"God, you know all the needs on this list, so I ask that you'll work in each situation. Be with Fred; let him know you haven't forgotten him even though his cancer has recurred. Father, may he feel your loving arms around him. Assure him of your presence no matter what the future holds. I pray you heal him, Lord, and let him stay with his young family. Meanwhile comfort him and his wife as only you can."

She touched the next name on the list. "Lord, be with little Molly. Give the doctors wisdom as they search for the cause of her ongoing stumbling . . ."

And on and on Aimee-Kate went until each person had been prayed for at length. Occasionally she paused to wipe away tears or to circle the names of people who had been on the list for a long time. Those were the ones to whom she'd send a card as a reminder they hadn't been forgotten.

Occasionally those who received a card from

Aimee-Kate would not only be encouraged but would tell others how much her notes and prayers meant to them. Eventually, and without meaning to, Aimee-Kate became known as a prayer warrior. She almost chuckled the first time someone called her that, saying she was too frail to be a "warrior" at anything. She certainly didn't consider what she did even a "ministry." Praying was just something she knew she could do. But what an encouragement the appreciative comments of those she prayed for were, especially when they cited times her prayers had made a difference not only in their situation but in their attitude. One man, who had been injured in a construction accident, said that when he didn't want to work hard in therapy, he'd think, *I have to keep at it; Aimee-Kate is praying.* As those kinds of reports got back to Aimee-Kate, she would think, *Well, maybe I'm not a total useless waste to God after all.*

Each week she called the church secretary for an update on the condition of those listed the previous Sunday or for the exact times patients would be undergoing medical tests. Then she prayed even more specifically. Sometimes her list was so long and the suffering so great that she became discouraged at the sheer numbers of hurting people. But each time she was tempted to stop praying for others, she would say, "Lord, just put your arms around the world, because I can't pray for everybody; I just know there's so much pain out there. But I trust you to help everyone—and me. So, thank you, Lord, for the gift of this day. Thank you that none of us is alone—not me nor the ones on this list. Help all of us to feel your reassuring presence."

One rainy afternoon after Aimee-Kate had finished her prayers with a quiet *amen*, she looked again at the picture of Jesus and the laughing girl. Then she closed her eyes, imagining Jesus hugging her—and the rest of the pitiful world—just as joyfully as he hugged the little girl. *Perhaps*, she thought, *there's a lot more hope for me than I realize.* She got up to look out the window at the big wide world, and she felt a new peace begin to grow inside her.

Chapter Six

"I Can't Do a Thing"

Wilma Picklesimer poured the pureed mixture of chicken and vegetables into a bowl, then touched a spoonful to her lips to test the temperature. Her sister, Adah Farley, had enough to contend with now that she was paralyzed; she didn't need a burned mouth too.

Adah had lived with Wilma and her husband for several years before the paralysis began. It first appeared as only a slight slowing of Adah's movements when she lifted a fork to her mouth. Then the day came when she couldn't push herself up from the table. A moment of panic crossed her face as she turned to a visiting young niece and said, "I can't move my arm." The little girl, with wide, frightened eyes, gently lifted Adah's uncooperative hand to the table-top, then let her aunt lean against her as she helped her stand. Adah tried to assure the child that the event had just been one of her "spells," but the next morning she fell as she got out of bed.

Wilma made a doctor's appointment immediately, and a wearying round to specialists began. Finally, at the University of Michigan, they received the dreaded diagnosis: Adah had progressive supranuclear palsy (PSP), which would gradually stiffen her muscles until she was totally paralyzed. "Just go home and put all your legal affairs in order," the doctor had said gently. Then he had added, "And don't put off any special trips you've wanted to take."

The next couple of years passed far too quickly, each month bringing more debilitation until Adah's condition forced her to a walker, then to a wheelchair, and finally to the bed. Adah's nieces and nephews remembered how they used to have trouble keeping up with this active woman when she escorted them to town. They missed her lessons in family history, given as she mended their blue jeans. Now her hands lay twisted and still upon the quilt covering her frail body. The contrast was so painful for many of the relatives that they stopped coming by, choosing instead to send another card that Wilma taped to the wall above Adah's railed bed.

Wilma, only two years younger and not in the best of health herself, took care of Adah—bathing her, turning her, feeding her, and trying to rub the achy pain out of a tired body that only vaguely resembled the woman her sister had once been. One day had been particularly difficult, and Adah managed to whisper apologetically, "I can't do a thing." Wilma patted her arm, fighting back tears as she said a silent prayer: *Lord, give me something encouraging to say.*

The answer came in a sudden brainstorm. "Adah, you can still pray," Wilma said. "Goodness knows this family needs plenty of that. Thea and the children left this morning for the Upper Peninsula. It's a long drive. Will you pray for them?"

Adah whispered, "I will."

During the next several weeks, each time Wilma received word of a particular need, she passed it along to her sister. When a neighbor mentioned that his brother was facing a series of complicated medical tests, Wilma assured him of her prayers. Then she added, "And I'll tell Adah too. She'll pray the whole time he's in the hospital. Do let us know how it goes."

A few days later the elated neighbor called. The doctors had decided his brother's problem could be controlled with medication. Surgery wouldn't be necessary after all.

When one of the men at church lost his job because the small company where he'd worked for twelve years closed, Wilma told Adah. The man found work the next month.

Gradually folks began to hear about Adah's constant prayers and began calling with requests. Sometimes a worried mother called about an ill child; sometimes a child called about an ailing pet. Once a gruff husband called, clearing his throat several times before finally saying that well, yes, he, uh, had heard that Adah was a praying woman. Would she, uh, pray for his marriage?

Day after day the requests came, and day after day Adah whispered her prayers. The time came, though, when her voice faded totally. When she didn't whisper her usual morning greeting, Wilma pulled the bed rail down to comfort her sister with a hug. Then she said, "Adah, even if you pray only in your mind, the Lord hears you." Adah nodded.

Then one morning as Wilma relayed yet another prayer request, Adah only stared at her, unable to nod her acknowledgment. Wilma closed her eyes briefly in her own silent prayer for all of her sister's suffering, then patted her on the arm. "That's okay, Adah. You just blink your eyes to answer me; one blink will mean yes, two blinks will mean no. Now, do you understand that Josie called to ask you to pray about moving her widowed mother?" Adah solemnly blinked once. Yes, she understood.

That was the beginning of Adah's third bedridden year, and her ministry continued for almost another year until God released her. Today when the relatives comment gratefully about her being free after years of painful paralysis, they also sorely miss her prayers. Sometimes they wonder aloud how those same prayers affected Adah herself. They couldn't help but notice that even in the midst of her pain, she possessed a graciousness and peace not expected from one so bound to a pain-filled body. Perhaps her concentration on others pulled her thoughts away from her own situation. Perhaps her constant prayerfulness wrapped her in God's grace. Or maybe just being in God's presence allowed her to transcend her circumstances. Whatever the reason for Adah's godly perseverance, her relatives and friends will always remember her for it and for the prayers that carried them all.

Praying for God's Work

God has given us prayer to have a realistic "work" that can be done in prison, in a wheelchair, in bed in a hospital or a hovel or a palace, on the march, in the midst of battle. . . . Astonishing? Unbelievable? But true. In Ephesians 6:10-20, the whole point is that the "armor of God" is needed to stand against, to wrestle against the "wiles of the devil." And it is there, in that context, that we are commanded to "pray always with all prayer and supplication in the Spirit." Prayer is not just icing on the cake of a so-called spiritual life; prayer is warm, close communication with the living God, and also a matter of doing an active work on His side of the battle.[6]

—EDITH SCHAEFFER

LOVE IN ACTION

May the Lord make your love increase and over-
flow for each other and for everyone else, just as
ours does for you.

1 THESSALONIANS 3:12

Dear friends, let us love one another, for love
comes from God. Everyone who loves has been
born of God and knows God. Whoever does not
love does not know God, because God is love.

1 JOHN 4:7-8

There are different kinds of gifts, but the same
Spirit. There are different kinds of service, but the
same Lord. There are different kinds of working,
but the same God works all of them in all men.

1 CORINTHIANS 12:4-6

The Little Things

God seems interested in little things. A widow's coin. The washing of a foot. The surrender of a small boy's loaves and fish.

He makes much of little things—as much as He wants to.

He may call us to move mountains once in a while, but the rest of the time He has plenty of molehills to be re-located. He probably wants more encouraging notes sent than books written, more sandwiches shared than sermons preached, more Band-Aids applied than edifices built.

That's good news for those of us who have only little things to work with.

Like a cup of water.

Or a chicken.

Or a word or deed so tiny it can't even be remembered—except by the recipient, who may never, ever forget.[7]

—JOHN DUCKWORTH

Chapter Seven

Silent Offerings

Bobbie stared at the dishcloth in her hand. *How could cotton material be so heavy?* she thought. She dropped it back into the sink. Wiping the countertop wasn't important anyway. Nothing was important now except her children, Marc and Lisa.

The house was filled with out-of-town relatives, new friends from church, and coworkers from the university. Someone had finished decorating the Christmas tree in the living room. Bobbie was having trouble sorting through all the chaos. How could her husband, her beloved Bill, have died? She still needed him. Their children needed him. How was she, a woman, going to raise ten-year-old Marc to be a man? And five-year-old Lisa looked absolutely lost as she wandered from room to room, looking for her dad and trying to make sense of all the strangers in the living room and kitchen. How could Bobbie explain Bill's absence to their children when she couldn't explain it to herself?

The four of them had moved to Mount Pleasant

less than six months ago for Bill to join the university faculty. They'd deliberately bought a house that would accommodate Bill's kidney dialysis machine. Now he was gone. Longtime friends, who would have provided a support base, were back in their former community. At least the general chaos here kept Bobbie's mind off the scary future. For now all she could do was finish the funeral arrangements and make sure Marc and Lisa were fed. The others in the house would have to fend for themselves.

Lisa came into the kitchen just then to tug at Bobbie's hand and pull her into the living room. All Bobbie wanted to do—in fact, all she had the energy to do—was sit on the sofa with her somber children, but there were phone calls to answer, decisions to make, and visitors to greet.

The only visitor either child was comfortable with was Christine, a young mother whose bright blue eyes sparkled with enthusiasm. Even though she lived across town, she often drove over during this stressful time to ask to take Lisa and Marc, and any other youngsters there, to the park for a romp.

Bobbie's thoughts wandered back several months to when Christine had invited her, Bill, and the children over to dinner shortly after their arrival in town. Christine's husband also taught at the university, and he had told her about Bill joining the faculty. That evening at Christine and Peter's, Bobbie had mentioned her nervousness as she was trying to get everything ready for Bill's parents' visit. Christine had pulled a package of spaghetti and a jar of sauce from her pantry. "Well, here's your first meal," she said as she held them up.

Bobbie remembered how they all had laughed then. How far away that fun evening now seemed with Bill's parents coming for a funeral and with a quiet Christine slipping into the house to take care of children or to bring order to the kitchen. If paper plates were sitting around, she'd gather them and then take out the garbage. If dirty dishes were in the sink, she'd wash them and put them away.

Some mornings she would slip quietly into the house, look around to see what needed to be done, and do it. She'd empty the clothes hamper, pick up any clothing on the bedroom floors, and take the laundry home so she wouldn't be adding to the chaos at Bobbie's house. Then a few hours later, she'd bring the clothing back, clean and folded, and put it where she thought it probably belonged.

One afternoon Bobbie noticed that their unmailed Christmas cards were still piled on the corner table. Bill had signed and addressed each one but left them unsealed. He had planned to do that the next day when he added the stamps. Bobbie glanced at them and murmured, "I've got to add a note to all those cards. How am I going to do that?" Christine immediately stepped forward to say, "I'll take care of those." She took the stack home, typed a message that Bill had died December 12, added stamps, and mailed the cards.

That entire week Christine quietly moved throughout the house, taking care of practical needs. Later, as Bobbie thought about Christine's silent offerings, she realized that the young mother had undoubtedly accomplished even more than what Bobbie had noticed. Most of all she had been God's messenger, bringing order not only to the household chaos but peace to Bobbie's weary spirit.

To Ponder:

Christine didn't ask how she could help; she just saw what needed to be done and did it. We care when someone is hurting—whether through a death in the family or an ongoing illness—and wish we could help. Many of us say sincerely, "Let me know if there's anything I can do." But most people in a crisis are not able to know what they need, much less verbalize it.

Next time someone you care about is in crisis, consider coming in behind the scenes to do what needs to be done. Sometimes we can have the greatest impact simply by our faithful, quiet activity.

Just Do It!

Your neighbor's child is diagnosed with a life-threatening illness. An older friend enters a nursing home. Chronic disease strikes a member of your family. A coworker has a heart attack.

What can you do to help?

Whether the person who is ill is a close friend, a relative, an acquaintance you don't know well but like a lot, or a coworker, it is natural to want to reach out, to make it better or at least to let her know you care. Yet often we are hesitant to act. We don't know what to do or are concerned we'll do the wrong thing. We don't want to intrude. We feel we might get in the way, or we assume the family has other people helping.

Sound familiar? Many of us have limiting thoughts that keep us from reaching out when we are truly needed.

What we heard again and again from both patients and their families was that any gesture is appreciated—from a greeting card, to making dinner, to some more creative ideas. It is truly the thought that counts.

The other message that came through loud and clear was "Just do it!" People in crisis are not able to give direction on things that need to be done. If they are lucky, a friend or relative is able to take charge, but more often the family just muddles through as best they can.[8]

—MARGARET COOKE

Chapter Eight

Umbrellas and Tulips

Kathy Hogan had waited with Diane's* husband and parents throughout the surgery and recovery time. Now she was in Diane's room, standing awkwardly near her bed, grateful for the opportunity to spoon ice chips through her friend's chapped lips. It gave her something tangible to do while waiting for the surgeon to bring the lab results.

Diane had battled breast cancer six years earlier but had been symptom-free until a few months ago, when she suffered with what the doctors thought was a kidney infection, then a kidney stone. But an MRI revealed fibrous tissues wrapped around the ureters, blocking kidney output and causing the infection. During the operation the surgeon peeled the tissue back bit by bit. When he got to the center, he found the suspicious mass, which was now being examined by the lab.

Suddenly the doctor was in the doorway. Kathy took one look at his face and knew he had bad news. Wanting Diane to have this time with her family, she said, "I'll be back soon," and slipped out into the hallway.

* Not her real name

As Kathy walked to the cafeteria, she thought of their friendship these past two years. She had enjoyed home schooling their children together, especially since Diane had so many interesting ideas, including taking all the kids to watch the counting of the votes after an election. *Well, those kinds of activities will have to be put on hold for a while,* Kathy thought. *But how can I help her now?*

A few years before, during Kathy's own hospitalization for pneumonia, she had been thrilled when her Sunday school class offered to bring meals for a week after she returned home. But they hadn't checked with each other, and every dinner for the next seven days was chicken-and-broccoli casserole! By the third evening, the family had gotten over their disappointment and were starting to be amused. By the seventh night, the humor had worn off, and the kids begged to have cold cereal. While Kathy certainly appreciated her friends' help, she would have enjoyed a greater variety.

Another time a woman had offered to help her after the birth of one of the children, but the woman's martyr attitude let Kathy know this was really a great inconvenience.

Now Kathy wanted her own help to be truly beneficial to Diane and her family. *Lord, help me be sensitive to Diane's needs,* she prayed. *I can't cure cancer, but I can do practical things. Please show me how to help.*

Kathy lingered over a cup of coffee before going back to Diane's room. She arrived just as the doctor was leaving and walked into stunned silence. The suspicious cells were indeed malignant. They had metastasized from the breast cancer six years earlier.

"I'm here for you, friend," was all Kathy could manage.

A few days later, when Diane was allowed to go home, she had to have nephrostomy tubes from her kidneys draining into collecting bags because of the cancer blocking the ureters. Most of her waking hours were spent resting in her easy chair with the tubes and bags hidden in shopping bags on each side of her chair.

Diane's parents stayed with her the first week she was home from the hospital. One afternoon Diane called Kathy and whispered, "Pray for me. Mom's throwing things out." Her mother, a highly organized, competent "neatnik," had decided to help Diane organize her home-schooling materials but was actually rather ruthlessly attacking the stacks of files, magazines, and brochures.

"I feel as though things are out of control," Diane said. "Especially since I know I can't home school this year. Just encourage me." So Kathy prayed with her right then on the phone.

But Kathy's encouragement didn't stop with prayer. The next afternoon she found two Scholastic

Aptitude Test books on a discount table at the bookstore. She grabbed one for her son, Matt, and then thought of Diane's son, Tim. She not only bought the second book for him but arranged to tutor him along with her own son for the upcoming SATs. In addition she picked up the applications for Tim to enroll along with Matt in the same junior college chemistry class.

Kathy wasn't finished yet. With the new round of chemotherapy, Diane's hair began to fall out, so Kathy called the American Cancer Society for a list of local businesses specializing in medical hair needs. One was just a mile away. That afternoon Kathy and her thirteen-year-old daughter, Kim, went shopping for head coverings. Wigs were too hot, and turbans weren't Diane's style, so Kathy chose a simple denim kerchief with a silver bang matching her friend's own prematurely silver hair. When they took it to Diane, she smiled and put it on immediately. Instantly she looked like the old Diane.

In addition to causing hair loss, the chemotherapy created huge sores inside Diane's mouth. Friends from church were bringing in meat dishes, which Diane's husband enjoyed but Diane couldn't eat.

One afternoon Kathy called and asked, "What do you have a taste for?" Diane didn't hesitate. "Pasta!" So Kathy made a pasta-and-cream-sauce dish while Kim created a frozen yogurt pie. The second night they took over cheese-stuffed pasta shells.

During this time Diane had to have a blood transfusion. Kathy, a universal donor (O negative), gave blood to her friend as well.

One afternoon Diane tried to express her appreciation. "I can't begin to tell you what it means that you have helped in so many practical ways. I won't ever be able to thank you." Kathy had merely patted her on the shoulder. "Diane, I can't cure cancer," she said. "But I can help with SATs and shop and cook and give blood. *That* I can do."

Kathy became too choked up to say more, but the next day she sent Diane a card depicting a tulip sheltered by an umbrella. The caption read, "God never meant for us to go through the tough times alone." Inside were the words, "That's why he gave us each other." Beneath that Kathy wrote, "I'm thankful for all the times through the years you've been the umbrella over *my* tulip." She paused for a long moment, then whispered, "Please, Lord," as she sealed the envelope.

———

To Ponder:

Everyone, regardless of individual talents, can be thoughtful and helpful to friends in need. Kathy would have liked to have done the miraculous in her friend's life, but since she couldn't, she looked for mundane and practical things she could do and thus provided a blessing.

What practical help can you provide for someone today?

Chapter Nine

Grandma's Newsletter

As Pat Johnson drove to the mall to buy her grandson a birthday present, she glanced toward snow-covered Pikes Peak rising majestically over Colorado Springs. The view was indeed beautiful, but she missed the Midwest. No, more specifically, she missed the Sunday dinners she had hosted back in Illinois for her six children, her husband's three children, and all the grandchildren. Pat missed hearing firsthand about newborn kittens and special programs at school, and she missed telling her relatives little things about her day too. Now everyone was spread from coast to coast.

Years ago she had found her mother's diary while cleaning out the old homestead and had been fascinated by the older woman's detailed recordings of her daily activities. Pat had lamented that she hadn't known those little pieces of her mother's life until her mom was gone. *That's what we should know about each other while we're alive,* Pat thought.

But how could she share all the parts of her life now when the family was so fragmented? And how could she keep them all connected? One grand-daughter had recently moved into her own apartment, and a little grandson was celebrating his fourth birthday. His parents had waited for him for-ever, it seemed. How could she remind the nine young adults that they were family—and that what touched one touched all? How could she let them know how much she loved each of them?

If only phone calls weren't so expensive. And writing each family member took forever. Deep in thought, Pat stopped at a red light. What she needed was a way to say everything she wanted to say for the price of a stamp. If only she could write *one* letter and send it to all nine of them. Wait! That was it! A newsletter would keep everyone connected, and she could add tidbits about her life too. She couldn't wait to find her grandson's gift and get back home. Within the hour she was in front of her computer.

Well, now. What do I say? Pat wondered. *Mom stuff*, she concluded and made a list of what to include: little daily events, a recipe or two the grandkids could help make, upcoming family birthdays and anniversaries (to encourage them to stay in touch with each other), suggestions for fun activities, a Bible verse to fit the season, crafts or word puzzles for the little ones, maybe household hints if she had room, news about each of them on a rotating basis. And, of course, she'd say "I love you" more than once. Finally she took a deep breath and began typing:

Time is flying! Here it is February already. I hope you've bought that valentine for your loved one. Be extra romantic this year. Send the kids to Grandma's and have a candlelit dinner at home. Put on your *Let Me Call You Sweetheart* album. Grill your favorite meat, use your best china, and linger! Talk to each other. Renew those tender dating days.

Okay, so Grandma is too far away, and the china is still packed in the basement. So put the TV in a child's bedroom, rent a good, two-hour movie for all the kids, order pizza for them, close the door, and voilà! you are alone.

For you singles, who knows, this may be the year your "Prince (or Princess) Charming" comes along. But remember, you need to be in the right place at the right time.

February is a great month to go roller-skating. Or if the weather isn't too cold, go ice-skating at a nearby pond. I remember as a child, I used to go up to the college in DeKalb and skate. Ice-skating makes me think of winter, and winter makes me think of skiing. And that makes me think, "When are the kids coming out to go skiing again?" How about it?! The slopes are beautiful. They have so much snow this year. Put those mittens in the car, fill it with gas, and get moving. The beds are clean, and the refrigerator is full.

Happy Birthday to Michael T. Szot, who will be four on February 14th. He's Grandma's valentine. Couldn't have asked for a better one!

After adding a Valentine's Day "Word Find," Pat signed off with:

Well, that's it, folks! Hope February is a wonderful month for you. Write when you can, call when you can, pray when you can, and always be good! I love you more than words can ever tell. You are all the joy of my life. Mom.

Within the next week, she was delighted by the response. Several of her nine adult children called, and each had family news she could include in the next newsletter. Now this was getting fun!

In the next mailing she gave a report of her trip with a friend to Kansas and an account of her husband's surprise sixty-fifth birthday party that included "Old Geezer" gifts and forced her to find new hiding places:

When I mixed the scalloped potatoes, I hid the pan in the dishwasher until time to bake. The buns were hidden in closets, and the big pan of baked beans was tucked behind the colas in the refrigerator.

If Pat occasionally gets busy and doesn't mail the newsletter out on time, family members call to check on the delay, adding more news. Amazingly, they even send each other a birthday or anniversary card occasionally. But most of all, they are reminded they are loved. And that's not bad for the price of a stamp.

"I Will Do More"

I will do more than belong, I will participate.

I will do more than care, I will help.

I will do more than believe, I will practice.

I will do more than be fair, I will be kind.

I will do more than forgive, I will love

I will do more than earn, I will enrich.

I will do more than teach, I will serve.

I will do more than live, I will grow.

I will do more than be friendly, I will be a friend.[9]

—DONNA PARTOW

SPIRITUAL STRENGTH

Trust in the LORD with all your heart
    and lean not on your own understanding;
in all your ways acknowledge him,
    and he will make your paths straight.

PROVERBS 3:5-6

I took you from the ends of the earth,
    from its farthest corners I called you.
I said, "You are my servant";
    I have chosen you and have not rejected you.
So do not fear, for I am with you;
    do not be dismayed, for I am your God.
I will strengthen you and help you;
    I will uphold you with my righteous right
        hand.

ISAIAH 41:9-10

I know what it is to be in need, and I know what
it is to have plenty. I have learned the secret of
being content in any and every situation, whether
well fed or hungry, whether living in plenty or in
want. I can do everything through him who gives
me strength.

PHILIPPIANS 4:12-13

A Spiritual Jump-Start

On the coldest days of the northern winter, we often find that our car battery has lost its charge during the night. The engine will not turn over because the battery is too weak. The ministry of encouragement is like a car that comes alongside ours and gives us a jump-start. The strength of the operative car is transferred into the weak battery, and the inoperative car is rejuvenated to action.

When we see people who are discouraged, saddened by the hardships of life, or simply tired of the Christian path of obedience, we need to come alongside and give them a spiritual jump-start. As Christ and other members of the Body of Christ strengthen us, we can strengthen others. By God's Holy Spirit, we can assist each other in the Christian life.[10]

—PAUL BORTHWICK

Chapter Ten

The Best Bargain

Doris Fay tried not to look at the clock; she had done that just a minute or two before . . . and three minutes before that. But her husband, Dave,* was late—again. She had called him before the end of his day to tell him she was cooking a pot roast—his favorite—and to ask if he could stop by the dry cleaners across the street from his office to pick up his shirts. But he had stammered something about needing to stay late to finish a report, and, of course, the cleaners would be closed by then. He also said not to wait dinner. He'd just grab something from the vending machine. No, no, not to worry. He'd be fine. Actually he was full from a late lunch.

Doris involuntarily stole another peek at the clock. It seemed Dave had a lot of special projects lately, but he said he couldn't very well refuse to stay, due to the downsizing of many of the departments. There were plenty of guys who'd be happy to, he said.

But something was wrong. Lately he didn't want to go for their after-dinner walks even when he did get

* Not his real name

72

home on time. And he was always hiding behind the newspaper. If she tried to engage him in conversation, he'd just mumble an answer.

Doris busied herself at the sink, scrubbing it for a second time. Just then she heard her mother-in-law, Betty, open the door from her area of the house. Doris smiled. It would be good to have Betty keep her company. She looked up just as the older woman entered the kitchen.

Betty paused at the solitary plate in Dave's customary spot. "He's still not home?" she asked.

Doris shook her head, then said, "When I called earlier, he said he'd probably have to stay late to finish that report . . ." Her voice trailed off.

Her mother-in-law looked at her sadly. "Doris, something is wrong, and you know it. I hate to say this against my own son, but Dave's not treating you right. I've sat right here and watched him ignore your questions about his day. And I never hear you two talk anymore. Used to be, I'd go to sleep listening to you laughing together."

Doris nodded, tears filling her eyes. "You're right, Mom. But whenever I try to talk to him about this, he just clams up."

Betty closed her eyes for a long moment, then stared hard at her daughter-in-law. "Doris, we're both praying about this separately," she said. "What if we started praying about it together? And I'm going to pray that the truth comes out. The *truth*, Doris—no matter what it is. Are you willing to pray that with me?"

Doris slumped for a moment against the cabinet, then turned again to look at Betty. "Yes," she answered. "I have a feeling I'm not going to like the answer, but I've got to know."

Betty nodded, sat down at the table, and patted the chair next to hers. For twenty minutes she and Doris talked to God, asking for the truth and for the strength to deal with whatever the situation was.

For the next several evenings, as Dave worked late, they continued their prayers. The crisis hit the following week when Doris answered the phone just as her husband lunged for it. At her "hello" the caller hung up. Doris took one look at her husband's face and suddenly knew. She tried to keep her voice calm. "You're having an affair, aren't you?" she asked.

Doris doesn't remember much about the hours that followed. She just remembers the stunned look on Dave's face as he started to deny her accusation but then shrugged and nodded. Doris felt as though cold water had been poured over her heart. Dave sighed with relief and resignation. "Well, I'm glad the truth is out," he said as he turned to go to the basement. Soon he came through the kitchen carrying his largest suitcase.

"I'll pack a few things tonight and be back for the rest this weekend," he said. "Better get a lawyer tomorrow morning."

The kitchen actually seemed to tip in that moment. Doris put her hand out to steady herself but stumbled into the nearest chair, too stunned to say anything. She could only watch numbly as Dave closed the front door behind him minutes later.

Soon Betty came into the room. She took one look at Doris's face and said sadly, "He's got another woman, doesn't he?" As Doris nodded mutely, Betty cradled her daughter-in-law's head against her abdomen and whispered softly, "Oh, I'm so sorry." Then with her arms still around Doris, she began to pray. "Lord, we asked for the truth, and you confirmed what we already knew but didn't want to face. Now please be with Doris—with all of us. Wrap your arms around her and give her your guidance and peace." Then the older woman's voice broke, and they sobbed together.

Dave refused Doris's pleas for counseling and reconciliation, so the next several weeks were awful as she told their children—they still had one son, a high school senior, at home—and then had to meet repeatedly with her new lawyer, who had a checklist of things to accomplish each week before the court date. Often Doris found herself staring at the list and thinking, *How do you condense all those years into this one list?* How did she and her husband—*ex-husband,* she realized—get to this point? She and Dave had served in church together. They'd taught Sunday school and worked with the youth together. They'd attended every marriage conference that came along. And now it had come down to a checklist.

Each morning as Doris awakened, she would have only a moment of peace before *he's gone* would shred through her spirit again. Suddenly she couldn't function, and even the most routine household chores would have remained untouched if Betty—in the midst of her own shock and declining health—hadn't taken over, making sure the laundry was done and meals were on the table. Often she'd have to urge Doris to eat "a little something" to keep up her strength. And always she was supportive of Doris and the children. She had tried to talk to Dave, but he refused to listen, saying, "I know everything you're going to say, Mom, and I don't want to hear it." The more Betty tried to remind her son of commitment, the greater the rift grew between them.

Doris and Betty prayed several times each day. Even though Doris was still moving in a zombielike state, she appreciated Betty's sense of balance as Betty stressed having things done in an honorable way that would please the Lord. But how, Doris wondered, does a person honor the Lord in the midst of something she is very much against? As she pondered that, she decided one way was to keep a calm spirit whenever she had to face Dave.

When the final decree was just days away, one of the lawyers raised the question of what to do with Betty. Her health was declining, and her only other option was to live with her daughter in another state. Doris was startled by the realization that she might lose her mother-in-law too. She turned to face Dave.

"Your mom's lived with us—with me—so long that I can't see uprooting her now. I'd like her to stay put if that's okay with you. If you want to pay rent for her to stay with me, I'd appreciate it."

And as easily as that, Doris was able to keep her mother-in-law as part of the divorce settlement.

Over the next two years, the two women were inseparable as Betty's health continued to decline. She was in and out of the hospital a number of times because of emphysema even though she had never smoked.

One evening, as Doris watched her gasp for breath, Betty managed, "I'm gonna die, aren't I?"

Startled, Doris fought back tears as she replied, "Well, Mom, we all are." Then she added, "But you know where you're going."

Betty suddenly smiled. "That's right. I do," she said. "And these ol' lungs will finally fill up."

For the next hour they talked about heaven and the relatives who would be there, as Doris occasionally stroked Betty's beautiful smooth cheeks framed by silver hair. How Doris would miss this woman's hearty laugh and her prayers. As Betty talked about her childhood, Doris thought about the little girl who was always interested in learning and who had grown up to teach Sunday school and tell numerous youngsters over the years about Jesus—the very one who would soon be welcoming her to heaven.

Just a few weeks later, Doris would hold that conversation close to her heart. When Betty took her last struggling breath, Doris suddenly had an image of her taking a deep breath in a beautiful garden—finally filling her lungs.

Later, as Doris listened to the preacher at Betty's funeral, she thought of the woman who had provided godly strength for her during the most difficult time of her life. Doris wondered what she herself would be remembered for. She hoped it would include persevering as Betty had done—and doing all the things that are important to keep a steady, faithful walk with the Lord.

Within her heart Doris whispered her good-byes: *Betty, you were the kind of woman who always got the job done. From you I learned the importance of prayer and Bible study and taking care of things I'm responsible for. Even now I can hear you telling our children, "When you've got something to take care of, do it." That's what you did, Betty; you took care of me. How I miss you! But I'll see you again.*

And with that thought, Doris dabbed at her eyes and then sat a little taller.

Chapter Eleven

Tissues and Common Sense

Margaret Bole picked up her sweater from the convention center bed, then opened her Bible to touch the photograph she carried of her eleven-year-old grandson Luke, pictured with his brother and parents shortly before he drowned.

"Oh, Luke, honey, your grandma misses you," she said aloud. "I know you're safe with Jesus, but I sure do miss your arms around my neck."

Margaret pulled a tissue out of her pocket and swiped at her eyes. "Now, Lord, I know you don't mind if I cry," she said. "But those women coming to the retreat prayer room today need someone who can listen to *their* hurts. I can't talk to hundreds of women like our speaker, and I can't sing like the musicians, but I can offer your hugs. So help me do that—and tell my little Luke that his grandma loves him."

Within a few minutes Margaret and her hostess, Harriett*—chair of the retreat—were downstairs,

* Not her real name

busily greeting the women who had come for the annual event. In the hours that followed, Margaret welcomed visitors to the prayer room with a warm smile, often gesturing toward the table where she had placed a small wooden cross bearing a red felt heart.

"We all need a place to hang our broken hearts, honey, so put it on the Cross," she'd often say. "After all, that's where his hung." As women quietly stammered their concerns, Margaret would say, "Now let's give that to Jesus together."

One after another the women told the sweet-faced woman the secrets of their hearts. Occasionally someone would refer to Margaret's "counseling," but she'd always shake her head. "I'm just praying with hurting women," she'd say as she dispensed tissues and common sense along with each prayer.

One young mother twisted her tissue into shreds while fighting tears. "My husband and I just got married two months ago," she managed. "We both lost our first spouses in accidents, so we suddenly have a blended family of four children under the age of seven. This past week was really rough. How are we ever going to raise these children?"

By now the young woman was sobbing against Margaret's shoulder. Margaret handed her another tissue, squeezed her hand, and said, "Honey, you're still grieving, and you're worried about your children to boot. As for how you'll raise them, you'll do as much as you can and then 'knee walk' the rest of the way. And every time you think you can't do this, just say, 'But God.' No one can carry all you have to carry—*but God* can."

Throughout that first evening, Margaret listened to, prayed with, and hugged several dozen women, who brought every kind of hurt to the prayer room. Then, just before the close of the evening's session, a young woman came in, almost pulling a teenage girl by the arm. The young woman introduced herself as a youth worker from one of the local churches. With her was seventeen-year-old Janet,* one of the young people in her group. Janet was a senior at the local high school but had not spoken since she was a young child. Doctors had no answers.

Margaret smiled and took Janet's hands, wondering—fearing—what awful trauma had touched this young woman, what unspeakable event had stunned her into silence for these many years. Margaret looked into green eyes set within a heart-shaped face surrounded by straight, shiny brown hair. The girl allowed Margaret to take her hands, but there was no enthusiasm in the touch. Margaret thought of her own little Luke, wondering what he would have been like as a teen. *Oh, Lord, why do awful things happen to children?* she asked silently.

Margaret invited Janet and her youth leader to sit on a nearby sofa with her. "God blessed me with three

* Not her real name

children," Margaret said. "I know what fun it is to have teenagers filling the house. What are your favorite activities?"

Immediately Margaret chided herself for asking a question of a teenager who didn't speak. But before she could apologize, Janet held up her hand in a "wait" signal and then dug around in her oversize bag to pull out a notepad and pen. Quickly she wrote a few words and thrust the pad toward Margaret, who read aloud, "Music and art."

Margaret smiled. "What type of music? What is your favorite group?"

Janet scribbled the name of a group that Margaret recognized as wailing depressing lyrics amid discordant melodies.

"I'm interested in why you like this group," Margaret said.

Janet shrugged, then wrote, "They see life the way I do."

Margaret took the girl's hands into her own. "Janet, honey, you've had professionals try to figure out why you don't talk, so I'm not going to pretend that I know. But I do know this: Jesus knows the answer, and he loves you."

Janet looked at her for a long moment, her eyes filled with bored politeness.

Margaret continued. "I've known you for only

these few moments, but I already love you. Will you let me pray for you?"

Janet shrugged, so Margaret bowed her head and began to talk to the God of the universe just as though he were someone who had stopped by for tea. She made no entreaties for instant healing or renewed faith on Janet's part; she just asked that Janet feel his love.

At her *amen,* Margaret looked up into green eyes that were watching her intently.

"Janet," Margaret said, "will you come back to see me tomorrow morning?"

Janet did exactly that. She also stopped in again at noon and in the afternoon. Each time, Margaret asked questions about her family. From the youth leader Margaret had learned that Janet's parents had recently divorced and that the mother left the children with the father.

At one point, as Margaret and Janet took a walk around the hotel grounds, Margaret asked, "Do you miss your mother?" Janet rocked her hand in a so-so gesture.

"Do you love her?" Margaret asked. The teen held up her hand to gesture again, but instead she nodded slowly. Margaret put her arm around the young woman's shoulders. "This is a lonely, difficult time for you, honey, but God hasn't forgotten you."

It was time for the last session, so Margaret hugged Janet before they went back into the building. "That hug's from me," Margaret said. Then she hugged the girl again, saying, "And that hug's from your mama. Your story isn't finished yet." This time Janet hugged her back.

After the retreat's closing details were taken care of, Margaret and Harriett plopped onto the sofa in Harriett's living room to recap the weekend. Margaret described Janet, then said, "Harriett, do you have any chocolate chips? I'd like to make cookies to take to her before I leave tomorrow."

Harriett smiled. "You're welcome to whatever I have."

The next morning, Margaret stood in the school hallway, waiting for Janet to pass between classes. When she saw the young woman, she waved, and Janet, grinning, hurried over to her. Margaret hugged her, then said. "Let's find a corner where we can talk for a moment."

As they stepped apart from the flow of students, Margaret wasted no words. "I brought you some cookies as a good-bye gift. I know you have to get to class, but I want you to know that I love you and I'm concerned about the music you're listening to. You're listening to the wrong music not only with your ears but also with your heart. Let God put a new song in your heart, honey."

Janet stared at her but did not nod her head. Margaret continued. "I'm going to write to you, and

I'll look forward to your answering. And occasionally I'll even call you."

At that, Janet frowned and shook her head. But Margaret continued. "Oh yes, I will. You can just tap your fingernails or a pencil against the receiver to give me your answers."

That was a new thought to the teen, and she looked amused. Margaret's eyes were filling with tears, so she hugged Janet good-bye and said, "We'll meet again, honey." For a long moment, Janet clung to her.

That afternoon on the plane, Margaret opened her worn Bible and again touched the picture of Luke. How she missed his infectious laugh. Suddenly she thought of the afternoon a neighbor boy had told him his older brother was joining God's army so he could tell others about God. Luke had chuckled at the news. "Oh, my grandma does that all the time," he'd said. "Everywhere she goes she tells people about Jesus."

Margaret smiled and thought, *Well, Luke, your grandma is still telling people about Jesus. And one of these days we'll see what God's going to do in Janet's life.* Then with her hand still on her open Bible, Margaret settled back and drifted off to sleep.

———

To Ponder:

Margaret wouldn't consider herself a spiritual giant, but her sensitivity to hurting women has allowed God to touch numerous lives through her, including that of a troubled, mute young woman with whom she still stays in touch.

God often uses ordinary women in extraordinary ways. Are you willing to let God love someone through you today?

Quiet Comfort

I was sitting, torn by grief. Someone came and talked to me of God's dealings of why it happened, of hope beyond the grave. He talked constantly, he said things I knew were true. I was unmoved except to wish he'd go away. He finally did. Another came and sat beside me. He just sat beside me for an hour and more, listened when I said something, answered briefly, prayed simply, left. I was moved. I was comforted. I hated to see him go.[11]

—JOSEPH BAYLY

Chapter Twelve

"Help Me Be Jesus"

Violet* stood with her hand still on the phone receiver long after her stepsister had said good-bye. The call had brought the news that her stepmother, Thetis,* had just been diagnosed with advanced colon cancer.

Violet eased into a nearby chair. She and Thetis had never been close, to say the least. How was she supposed to respond to this? She leaned back in her chair, remembering. She had been thirteen years old when her widowed father had remarried, and he had chosen Thetis, a young girl near her own age whom Violet couldn't stand. She had tried to talk her father out of marrying Thetis, but he had dismissed her concern, saying her mother was dead and wasn't coming back, so he needed to get on with living. Then he dropped the threat: "And I expect you to get along with Thetis. Like it or not, she's going to be your new mother. If you can't get along with her, you'd better find someplace else to live."

* Not their real names

And that's exactly what Violet chose to do a few months later, after Thetis stole her first paycheck from her after-school job at the town diner. Violet remembered the afternoon she had grabbed a paper sack from under the sink and ran to her room to gather her few garments and her mother's old-fashioned tortoiseshell hair combs. Violet hurried past her smirking stepmother, and within a few minutes she was knocking at her boss's door. Could she rent the furnished room attached to the diner? In small-town environments during the early 1940s, it wasn't all that uncommon for boys and girls as young as Violet to be on their own.

Over the next couple of years, Violet was especially lonely when she'd see her father or Thetis downtown with their babies. But she'd merely nod to them. She had her own life now, and her new friends helped her bury the painful past.

About this time Violet's uncle started a church in his garage and invited her to attend. But she preferred her own crowd—especially Roger, a soldier she had met at a party. Within a few months of that first meeting, they eloped. Then, just a few weeks after her seventeenth birthday, Violet realized she was pregnant. Her twin boys were born in December of that year.

Her new responsibilities suddenly made her ready to listen to her preacher uncle. She certainly wanted her sons to have a more stable home than she had known, so she started attending the garage church. As she listened week after week, she became less aware of the lingering smell of car exhaust and grease and more aware of the words about messed up and meaningless lives. Finally one Sunday she knelt with her uncle at the front row of folding chairs and asked the Lord to be her Savior. Then the strangest thing happened: As she prayed for God's forgiveness, she suddenly knew in some inexplicable way that she had to forgive Thetis and her father for their unloving actions.

That forgiveness didn't come overnight, but as she kept asking for the Lord's help, she knew she had no choice but to forgive if she wanted her children to have a good relationship with their grandparents—something she knew she'd missed in her own life. Finally she took a deep breath and prayed, "Okay, Lord, I'll extend the dinner invitations; you provide the forgiveness."

Over the next year, Violet—often with her jaw set—invited her father, Thetis, and their two children to every family celebration. For the sake of the grandchildren, they came. Gradually it began to take less effort to welcome them. During the next several years, any observer would have been impressed with the apparent closeness of the two families.

Then Violet's father died of cancer. After the funeral service Violet put her hand on Thetis's arm.

"I'm sorry you're having to go through this," she said. Thetis merely stared at her for a long moment before saying, "Don't come snooping around expecting to get anything. You were already raised by the time we got married, so everything is coming to me and my children."

Violet, stunned, stared back at her. She wasn't interested in money; she was sharing Thetis's grief. And "already raised"? At thirteen? The old hurts threatened to sweep away the progress she'd made in forgiving the past.

"He never did anything for me when I was alive," Violet answered. "I don't expect anything now." And she turned and walked away.

In the years that followed, Violet sent occasional cards on birthdays and holidays, but she didn't see Thetis. Now, a decade later, Violet was experiencing new emotional turmoil. How did God expect her to respond now that Thetis had cancer and was in need? Thetis's children had moved to other states and were busy with their own lives and families; only Violet was close enough to provide practical help.

"Lord, I need your guidance," Violet whispered. "I know you've forgiven all my sins, so I'm supposed to forgive others. But how do you want me involved here? It would be so easy just to ignore her; after all, she certainly did that—and more—to me. My heart still hurts; I can't offer to help her in my own strength."

As she spoke, she stared at the crusted skin on her index finger where she had bumped a hot skillet the previous week. She sighed, then whispered again, "Lord, I trust you, though, to heal my heart just as you are healing this burned finger. Day by day, as new skin is covering my knuckle, I trust you to help me concentrate on the good in my life now and not on the wrong that was done to me then. And help me be Jesus to this woman who has no one to care for her."

That afternoon, Violet went to see Thetis. She got right to the point. "Thetis, you're going to need somebody to help you with your medicines and meals and such. I want you to come and live with us so I can take care of you until you get better."

Thetis looked cross and perplexed. "Why would you do that?" she challenged.

"Because it's the right thing to do," Violet answered. "God forgave me when he gave me eternal life. Part of my forgiving you is to take care of you now."

Thetis's eyes snapped. "There's nothing to forgive me for!"

Violet's expression never changed. "I'd like you to stay with us until you're well."

Thetis paused, then looked around her living room. "No, I want to be with my own stuff."

93

Violet stood to go. "Well then, I guess I'll just have to come here." And for the next three months, Violet appeared on Thetis's doorstep each morning.

At first Violet merely dispensed the medications, prepared a hearty soup, and did laundry or dusted. As the cancer progressed, however, Violet's visits grew longer. She changed the bed linens daily and even fed Thetis each meal. And always she talked about the difference the Lord had made in her life.

One day she asked Thetis outright, "Have you ever given your heart to Jesus?" Thetis nodded and said, "Yes, just the other day."

And that was that. Thetis never mentioned her faith again, but it began to show in a softer nature. Then one day when a visitor stopped in, Thetis introduced Violet with "This is my daughter," not with her usual snide label of "step." When Thetis died just a few days later, Violet was at her side, holding her hand.

———————

To Ponder:

When you have been treated poorly, you still can become God's instrument in the life of someone who doesn't "deserve" your love—not because you are strong and "saintly," but because you let him be strong through you.

Are you willing to extend love and forgiveness to people who have hurt you, even if they don't ask for that forgiveness? Do you need to ask forgiveness of someone you've hurt?

Bits and Pieces

Anne Morrow Lindbergh observed somewhere in her timeless little book, *Gift from the Sea,* that most of us don't really mind pouring our lives out for a reason. What we do resent is the feeling that it is being dribbled away in small, meaningless drops for no good reason.

For me, one of the greatest frustrations of walking through the "dailiness" of my life as a Christian is that I don't always get to see how the bits and pieces of who I am fit into the big picture of God's plan. It's tempting at times to see my life as a meal here, a meeting there, a carpool, a phone call, a sack of groceries—all disjointed fragments of mothering in particular.

And yet I know I am called, as God's child, to believe by faith that they do add up. That in some way every single scrap of my life, every step and every struggle, is in the process of being fitted together into God's huge and perfect pattern for good.[12]

—CLAIRE CLONINGER

MOTHER LOVE

Her children arise and call her blessed;
  her husband also, and he praises her.

PROVERBS 31:28

As a mother comforts her child,
  so will I comfort you.

ISAIAH 66:13

Only be careful, and watch yourselves closely so that you do not forget the things your eyes have seen or let them slip from your heart as long as you live. Teach them to your children and to their children after them.

DEUTERONOMY 4:9

Guardians of the Future

Women with children at home are guardians of a future generation. Those boys and girls will become the business leaders, doctors, judges, missionaries, preachers, musicians, teachers, and political leaders of the future. The kind of people they will someday become is directly related to the commitment you make to them now. If you don't dedicate yourself to raising them, to giving them moral standards and Christian values, who will? Mothering is the single most significant thing most of us will ever do.[13]

—VICKIE KRAFT

Chapter Thirteen

Lavender Memories

As Cotha Prior strolled past the new shop that sold body lotions and soaps, the lavender-wrapped bars displayed in the window caught her attention. Her daughter, Monica, would like those. Once inside, Cotha picked up the closest bar and held it to her nose. The fragrance carried her back to her childhood.

She remembered Margie, the little girl in her fifth-grade class who always was poorly dressed and whose bathing habits were, well, not one of her regular habits. Even at that young age, Cotha knew how important the opinions of her friends were, so although she felt sorry for Margie, she couldn't risk being friends with her.

Then one afternoon, as the young Cotha colored the states on her homework worksheet, she casually mentioned Margie to her mother, who stopped in the middle of stirring the stew to ask, "What's her family like?"

Cotha didn't look up. "Oh, really poor, I guess," she answered.

"Well, it sounds as though she needs a friend," Mrs. Burnett said. "Why don't you invite her to spend Friday night with you?"

Cotha looked up quickly then. "You mean *here?* Spend the night with me? But, Mom, she *smells.*"

"Cotha Helen." Her mother's use of both names meant the situation was settled. There was nothing to do but invite Margie home. The next morning Cotha hesitantly whispered the invitation at the end of recess while her friends were hanging up their jackets and combing their hair. Margie looked suspicious, so Cotha added, "My mother said it's okay. Here's a note from my mother to give to yours."

So two days later they rode the school bus home while Cotha tried to ignore the surprised looks on her friends' faces as they saw the two of them together. Have two fifth-grade girls ever been quieter? Cotha thought of other times when she'd been invited to spend the night with a friend. They would talk and giggle all the way to their stop.

Finally Cotha gave a determined little huff and said to Margie, "I've got a cat. She's going to have kittens."

Margie's eyes lit up. "Oh, I like cats." Then she frowned as though recalling a painful memory and added, "But my dad doesn't."

Cotha didn't know what to say then, so she feigned interest in something outside the school bus window.

Both girls were silent until the bus rolled to a stop in front of the white house with the green shutters.

Mrs. Burnett was in the kitchen. She greeted Cotha and Margie warmly and then gestured toward the table set with two glasses of milk and banana bread. "Why don't you girls have a little snack while I tend to dinner," she said.

When the banana bread was finished, Mrs. Burnett handed each child identical paper-doll books and blunted scissors. Dressing the paper women in shiny dresses gave them something in common to talk about. By the time they washed their hands for dinner, they were chatting enthusiastically about school.

After the dishes were done, Mrs. Burnett said, "Time to take a bath before bed, girls." Then she held out scented soaps wrapped in lavender paper. "Since this is a special night, I thought you might like to use fancy soaps," she said. "Cotha, you first, and I'll wash your back for you."

Then it was Margie's turn. If she was nervous about having an adult bathe her, she didn't show it. As the tub filled, Mrs. Burnett poured in a double capful of her own guarded bubble bath. "Don't you just love bubble bath, Margie?" she asked as though the child bathed in such luxury every day.

She turned to pull Margie's grimy dress over her head, then said, "I'll look away as you take the other things off, but be careful climbing into the tub. That brand of bubble bath makes it slippery."

Once Margie was settled into the warm water, Mrs. Burnett knelt down and soaped the wet washcloth heavily before rubbing it over the child's back.

"Oh, that feels good," was all Margie said.

Mrs. Burnett chatted about how quickly Cotha and Margie were growing and what lovely young women they were already. Repeatedly she soaped the washcloth and scrubbed Margie's gray skin until it shone pink.

Through the whole thing Cotha was thinking, *Oh, how can she do that? Margie is so dirty.* But Mrs. Burnett continued to scrub cheerfully, then washed Margie's hair several times. Once Margie was out of the tub, Mrs. Burnett dried her back and dusted her thin shoulders with scented talcum. Then, since Margie had brought no nightclothes, Mrs. Burnett pulled one of Cotha's clean nightgowns over Margie's now shining head.

After tucking both girls under quilts, Mrs. Burnett leaned over to gently kiss them good night. Margie beamed. As Mrs. Burnett whispered, "Good night, girls," and turned out the light, Margie pulled the clean sheets to her nose and breathed deeply. Then she fell asleep almost immediately.

Cotha was amazed that her new friend fell asleep

so quickly; she was used to talking and giggling for a long time with her other friends. To the sound of Margie's gentle breathing, Cotha stared at the shadows on the walls, thinking about all her mother had done. During Margie's bath, Mrs. Burnett had never once said anything to embarrass the girl, and she'd never even commented about how grimy the tub was afterward. She just scrubbed it out, quietly humming the whole time. Somehow Cotha knew her mother had washed more than Margie's dingy skin.

All these years later, the adult Cotha stood in the fragrant store, the lavender soap still in her hand, wondering where Margie was now. Margie had never mentioned Cotha's mother's ministrations, but Cotha had noticed a difference in the girl. Not only did Margie start coming to school clean and pleasant on the outside, but she had an inside sparkle that came, perhaps, from knowing someone cared. For the rest of the school year, Cotha and Margie played at recess and ate lunch together. When Margie's family moved at the end of the school year, Cotha never heard from her again, but she knew they had both been influenced by her mother's behavior.

Cotha smiled, then picked up a second bar of the lavender soap. She'd send that one to her mother, with a letter saying that she remembered what her mom had done all those years ago—not only for Margie but for Cotha as well.

Chapter Fourteen

Moving On

Sarah* sighed as she stood in the doorway of the furniture-cluttered bedroom she had shared with her husband, Don. It had been fifteen months since his death from brain cancer, but Sarah was only now realizing how crowded the room was with her bed next to the one he had used during his illness. After the funeral she had ignored the other bed—and the resulting clutter.

Suddenly she'd decided this overcast morning it was time to turn the bedroom from "theirs" into "hers," so with her eleven-year-old son's help, she tackled the chore with determination. About an hour into the job, the phone rang. It was her mother, Willa.*

"You sound out of breath, honey," the older woman said. "Did you have to run up the stairs to answer?"

"No. John* and I were just shoving furniture around," Sarah answered. "I've taken down the single bed and was rearranging my bedroom."

* Not their real names

Sarah could hear her mother crying softly.

"What's wrong?" she asked.

No answer. Just more sniffs.

"Mother, please don't do that," Sarah pleaded. "You know I can't stand it when you cry long distance. I'm only rearranging furniture."

Finally her mother could talk. "It's just that the Lord answered my prayer," she said. "When I was out there last month and helped you fold the laundry, I looked at that crowded room and asked the Lord to help you move on. And every morning since then I've asked him to nudge you to rearrange that room."

That startled Sarah, of course, but it also got her to thinking. What if her mother had marched into her home and announced, "Okay, you've ignored this room long enough. It's time to get on with your life!" Obviously it wouldn't have worked since the "letting go" would have been in response to another's insistence rather than to Sarah's own readiness.

Throughout the day, as Sarah put the finishing touches on "her" bedroom, she smiled when she thought of her mother, a wise woman who chose to patiently offer emotional support while trusting the Lord to move her daughter forward.

———

To Ponder:

Mothering is the most difficult job in the world. To see a child's emotional hurt and to ache for that child while quietly and prayerfully restraining the impulse to control and "fix" is another way to serve God. Do you need to turn your children over to God in this way?

Chapter Fifteen

Yes, She Can!

Judy's mother, Anita Sutton, snapped photo after photo of Judy in her college graduation gown, both before the commencement ceremony and as Judy celebrated with numerous relatives and enjoyed her congratulatory cake afterward.

Anita and her husband never stopped smiling. Finally they pulled their daughter into the kitchen, still grinning. "We have something we want you to know, and then we'll tell why we waited until now," her mother said.

Judy, bewildered, looked at her mother's shining face. Her parents glanced at each other, pride and excitement evident in their eyes. Anita turned back to Judy and put her hands on the young woman's shoulders.

"Judy, honey, when you were in junior high, your class took some standardized tests ordered by the school district. When the results came back, we were called to the counselor's office and told, 'You should know that, based on your daughter's test scores, she probably will never graduate from high school.'"

Anita continued, "Of course we were stunned, but we decided not to tell you because we didn't want you to get it into your head that you couldn't graduate. Instead we decided to do everything in our power to help you do the best you could."

Judy frowned. "Did they think I was retarded or something?"

Her mother shook her head. "They based everything on those low scores. But we didn't want that test determining your future, so we told the counselor he must never show you the results. Then I got a little feisty and told him you *would* graduate—not only from high school but from college too."

As Judy listened, memories darted across her mind of all her parents had done to help her study during high school. She'd had a difficult time with some of her classes, but every afternoon her mother had helped her study, and her father had tutored her in math. Judy thought of all the hours that must have taken—especially since there were three other children in the family whose homework had to be supervised.

Judy's mind whirled as her mother continued. "The reason we waited until now to tell you was that we didn't want you to hit a discouraging time in college and say, 'Well, why should I finish? I wasn't expected even to finish high school.' We probably never would have told you at all if you hadn't decided to be a teacher," her mother said. "But we knew we had to tell you now so you wouldn't make that counselor's same mistake and tell parents their child couldn't do something. We want you to be optimistic about every child's potential and suggest positive, concrete ways parents can help. We're proud of you, honey. You proved those test givers wrong!"

Judy's eyes filled with tears as she hugged her parents and managed to whisper a hoarse "Thank you."

In the years that followed, Judy carried the scene with her. She was grateful for her mother's encouraging words that didn't stop at graduation but strengthened her throughout a successful teaching career, marriage, and motherhood. Judy also watched her mother encourage others. Anita was a steady sounding board when people were faced with a difficult decision. Many of them just needed a dose of her basic optimism that said things were going to turn out okay. Anita's optimism rubbed off on Judy too, often making a difference in Judy's attitude toward her students and, later, her own three children.

Today Judy is married to a chaplain with the California Youth Authority. In addition to her work as assistant pastor of care ministries at a large church, she is solidly pursuing an M.A. degree in pastoral care and counseling. She loves pointing out the strengths of those who feel as though they have no gifts and suggesting ways they can use their talents for ministry. And to think it all started with Judy's mother's refusal to let a school counselor's negative assessment hold her daughter back.

To Ponder:

It doesn't take an extraordinary mother to believe in her child or to devote herself to helping that child overcome obstacles. It just takes love and a big dose of determination. Can you supply some of both for your child today?

A Grand Task

Work should always be associated with joy. . . .

The story is told of three women washing clothes. A passerby asked each what she was doing.

"Washing clothes" was the first answer.

"A bit of household drudgery" was the second.

"I'm mothering three young children who someday will fill important and useful spheres in life, and wash-day is a part of my grand task in caring for these souls who shall live forever" was the third.

Ordinary work, which is what most of us do most of the time, is ordained by God every bit as much as is the extraordinary. All work done for God is spiritual work and therefore not merely a duty but a holy privilege.[14]

—ELISABETH ELLIOT

MENTORING

Do not let any unwholesome talk come out of your mouths, but only what is helpful for building others up according to their needs, that it may benefit those who listen.

EPHESIANS 4:29

Teach the older women to be reverent in the way they live, not to be slanderers or addicted to much wine, but to teach what is good. Then they can train the younger women to love their husbands and children, to be self-controlled and pure, to be busy at home, to be kind, and to be subject to their husbands, so that no one will malign the word of God.

TITUS 2:3-5

Let the word of Christ dwell in you richly as you teach and admonish one another with all wisdom, and as you sing psalms, hymns and spiritual songs with gratitude in your hearts to God.

COLOSSIANS 3:16

Too Small for God?

Have you ever felt insignificant? Too small to make a difference in this immense world of need? . . .

Do we believe in a personal God who uses broken, limited and overwhelmed people to do his will in the earth? Do we believe in the God of "mustard seed" faith, who does great things through what appear to be insignificant means? Do we believe Paul's words to the Corinthians, that God chooses "the foolish things of the world to shame the wise . . . the weak things of the world to shame the strong" (1 Cor. 1:27)? . . .

If you see yourself as small, insignificant or overwhelmed, take courage: you are exactly the humble kind of person God wants to use mightily in the world. . . . (1 Pet. 5:5-6) . . .

. . . God uses ordinary people who make themselves available to him. Comprehending this allows us to enter the world with hope. As we remember the biblical accounts of how God changed the world through cowards, shepherds and impulsive fishermen, we will start asking, "OK, Lord, how do you want to use me in this broken world?"[15]

—PAUL BORTHWICK

Chapter Sixteen

The Extra Mile

Suzanne Rasnick let out an exasperated huff as she studied the classified ads. It was ridiculous that she was having to look for a job. She was raised to be a full-time wife and mother, and she had been doing exactly that until she found herself facing an unwanted divorce. Now she was thrust into a world where she was convinced she didn't belong. She hadn't worked outside her home in years. What could she possibly do that would allow her to interact with people beyond smiling at them from behind a cash register?

Well, here is something interesting, she thought as an ad caught her eye. Her city government had a public relations opening. That would be something she'd like—bragging about her town and getting folks interested in coming to see what was happening here. *But can I do that?* she wondered. After all, she'd only had occasional stints as a volunteer for the past twenty years. "Who would ever hire me after all that time of baking cookies and running carpools?" she asked aloud. The cat, her only audience, blinked sleepily at her.

For the next two mornings, Suzanne continued to scan the classifieds as soon as her three children left for school. She found that she kept turning back to the job listed with the city government. *Lord, what should I do?* she prayed. The thought *At least look into it* settled into her mind, but it still took her two more days before she gathered the courage to call for an appointment.

As Suzanne carefully dressed the next morning, she didn't know the city council had just decided not to fill the advertised position. By the time she arrived for her appointment, the personnel director had scrambled to find another position to talk to her about. Would she be interested in working for six weeks as an assistant to the director of tourism? The director had been in an accident and needed that time to recuperate. Somebody had to be in place immediately to welcome the Kentucky Press Association for their annual conference.

Suzanne smiled. "Sure, welcoming visitors is something I can do," she said. So within the week she met numerous people, including Gerri Kinder, the director of external affairs and coordinator of publications at nearby Pikeville College. As they chatted briefly, Gerri asked Suzanne if she had any writing experience.

"Well, yes, I've done a little," she answered. "I was president of my daughter's high school band boosters and wrote the monthly newsletter."

Gerri nodded. "That's good. Stop by and see me when this temporary assignment is over."

A few weeks later Suzanne was in Gerri's office, showing her the newsletters and short stories she had written. But even though Suzanne needed a job, she still panicked when Gerri offered to have her write the college newsletter.

"Let me think about this," Suzanne said. "I don't even know how to turn on a computer, let alone use one."

"You think about it," Gerri said. "I'll call you tomorrow."

That night, as Suzanne pondered the offer, she decided she couldn't do it. What made her think she could ever do anything that important? Smiling at folks was one thing, but the baffling computer world was another. No, she decided, she couldn't do it. She fell into a fitful sleep.

The next morning Gerri called. She got right to the point: "Have you decided yet?"

"Well, yes, I have," Suzanne replied. "I'm not going to take it. I'll never be able to do all that computer stuff."

Suzanne expected Gerri to sign off then with a typical, "Thanks for thinking about it." Instead Gerri chuckled. "Well, I believe you *can* do this. Tell you what. Try it for thirty days. If at the end of that time you're still uncomfortable, then you can go with my blessing." Gerri continued, "You *can* learn to use the computer— it just *looks* scary—and I'll teach you. It's what can't be taught that I want: your ideas and creativity."

So that's how Suzanne wound up sitting in front of a computer with Gerri standing beside her, ready to point out the keys that would unlock the vast mysteries of cyberspace. But as she positioned herself before the screen, Suzanne suddenly panicked. "What if I tear it up?" she asked. "What if I destroy its brain?"

Gerri stifled a guffaw. "We have people who fix them," she replied. "Now, let's get started. You're not going to kill it, so take a deep breath and relax."

Gradually, under Gerri's tutelage, Suzanne gained ever-increasing levels of expertise. During the next two years, not only did Suzanne successfully write the newsletter, but she also wrote college ad campaigns and press releases, planned highway billboard displays, and managed radio and TV advertising. All the while, Gerri encouraged her creativity. "Don't hold back," she'd say to Suzanne. "Spread your wings. Have fun with this."

And she did. Suzanne's confidence grew mightily under Gerri's praise. Slowly she began to realize that she could do far more than she had ever believed. Oh, Gerri would correct her as well, but her comments were always sandwiched between praise.

As the second anniversary of Suzanne's hiring approached, the director of tourism moved away. When Suzanne saw the posted job notice, something stirred within her. That morning she casually mentioned to Gerri that she'd seen the posting. "Yes, I saw it this morning too," Gerri said. "I thought of you right away. It's a perfect fit, you know. Why don't we just pray about it now?" Together they asked for the Lord's direction.

When Suzanne became the director of tourism for Pike County, she knew that no matter where her career took her, she owed much to the woman who went the extra mile to help her make the transition from home to the workplace. Not only did Gerri encourage her creativity, but she also showed her how to turn on a computer without destroying its "brain."

To Ponder:

Gerri went beyond her professional responsibility to offer the training and encouragement she knew Suzanne needed. And in the process, she helped Suzanne grow into the person God wanted her to be.

Encouraging or mentoring someone doesn't take a great talent or gift, but it can change a life. Will you ask God to bring someone across your path who needs to be encouraged or motivated?

Chapter Seventeen

The Welcome Date

Lori Miller smiled as the doorbell rang. That would be Tim, right on time as always. She hurried to open the door. No time to stall tonight. This was the evening she would be meeting his parents for the first time, and she was as nervous as could be. *What if I drop salad in my lap at dinner?* she worried. *What if his mother hates me?*

During the thirty-minute drive in Southern California traffic, Lori tried to cover her nervousness by chatting about their responsibilities in the same mortgage company. In the pauses Tim wondered aloud what his mother would fix for dinner. Probably her spicy chicken, he finally decided.

They were running late, but it seemed to Lori that the drive was over too quickly when Tim pulled up in front of a stucco house with red flowering bushes tumbling toward the sidewalk. As Tim opened Lori's car door, he grinned. "Hey, I can smell dinner all the way out here," he said. "It's her spicy chicken, all right."

Lori tried to mirror Tim's enthusiasm, but she

glanced nervously toward the front walk, wishing Tim would comment on how she looked.

As they approached the door, Tim's mother, Patricia, came to the front stoop and met them with a beautiful smile. As she hugged Tim in greeting, she teased him. "I was beginning to think I'd have to throw out dinner," she said.

Tim was quick with his retort: "Ah, Ma, I'd just go digging in the garbage to get your cooking."

Then Patricia turned to smile at Lori. "Welcome! I hope you like chicken," she said.

Lori smiled back. "I do. Tim was hoping you'd make that tonight. He says it's the best around."

As Patricia beamed at the compliment, her husband, Roy, appeared behind her, greeting Tim and Lori warmly. After hors d'oeuvres, the four gathered around the dinner table, where Tim leaned forward to breathe in the aroma from the steaming serving platter. Lori unfolded her napkin, ready to sample this dish Tim had raved about. Instead, the others extended their hands toward each other. Lori, in bewilderment, offered hers as well. The family bowed their heads, and Patricia began to pray. Lori quickly bowed her head too, but she was only vaguely aware of the words thanking the Lord for Tim and Lori's safe drive and asking him to bless the food and their time together. At Patricia's "In the name of your Son, Jesus, Amen,"

Lori looked up, still in shock. No one seemed to notice though, and Patricia handed her the serving platter as she asked about Lori's job.

The rest of the evening was uneventful as they ate and played table games. Lori enjoyed the banter, but she continued to ponder Patricia's prayer. Suddenly she was more than a little frightened by this tall woman with the big blue eyes and reddish hair. Lori couldn't wait to talk to Tim at the end of the evening.

They had barely pulled away from the curb when Lori asked, "How come you didn't tell me about your mother."

Tim looked bewildered. "What do you mean?"

"I mean that your mother prayed before the meal—and we held hands!" Lori exclaimed.

Now Tim looked even more baffled. "We always do that," he said. "I didn't think it was a big deal."

Well, it was a big deal to Lori, and she settled back against the seat to think about it. The closest she could come to explaining the feeling even to herself was that she had just seen a bright light. She knew she was missing something in her life, but she didn't know what. While she couldn't explain her discomfort, fear was the closest word she could find to describe what she felt.

As Tim and Lori continued to date, Lori cautiously accepted Patricia's friendship, even welcoming her invitation to an Easter sunrise service. That morning reminded her of long-ago childhood days when she and her family had attended church together. While she listened to the music and the sermon, she realized that she gradually was losing her fear of Patricia and was beginning to appreciate that Patricia lived what she said she believed.

Then one evening Patricia called Lori at home. "Our church is sponsoring a conference in Culver City," she said. "Tim has to be out of town that weekend, but if you're interested, I'd like you to go as my guest. The speaker is funny, but he sticks to the gospel."

Lori wasn't exactly sure what "sticks to the gospel" meant, but if Patricia was endorsing the event, she knew it would be good. Besides, it would be interesting to get answers to some of her questions.

As it turned out, Lori got more than answers to her questions; she accepted the Lord. Finally she understood the reason behind Patricia's confidence. Now, not only was she not afraid of this woman, but Lori even started to stay at their house on occasional Saturday nights in order to go to church the next morning with her friend—even if Tim didn't go.

One Sunday morning the minister talked about the importance of making sure every relationship was from the Lord. Suddenly Lori's eyes filled with tears; she knew she and Tim were not for each other. Tim knew it, too, but Lori had been so afraid of losing Patricia's friendship that she hadn't wanted to face the truth. On the way home from church, Lori cried as she told Patricia she and Tim were going separate ways. "We've both known that needed to happen, but I didn't want to lose you," Lori managed.

Patricia nodded. "I've seen this coming," she said. "But just because you won't be dating Tim doesn't mean you and I can't continue our friendship. We can still meet for lunch and talk on the phone. Think of it this way: God put Tim in your life temporarily so you and I could meet."

Knowing she wouldn't lose Patricia, too, helped Lori adjust to the inevitable parting with Tim. Today Lori is happily married and very much aware of God's hand upon her life. And all because a smiling woman welcomed her son's date.

To Ponder:

Patricia is not an extraordinary woman doing spectacular works for God. But she is making a difference just by being a godly example, reaching out to others and loving them into God's kingdom. Are you willing to let God bring someone into your life who needs to see Jesus?

A Few Good Women

Can you really make a difference? Do the things you say and do really matter? God's Word answers a resounding "yes" to these questions. He's looking for a few women who will bring light to this dark world—people He can use to change the course of history. But in order to change others, you have to start with your own life. Being a Christian is more than going to church. It's developing a relationship with your Heavenly Father. It's becoming more like Jesus every day.[16]

—BRAD HUMPHREY

Chapter Eighteen

"Call Dinny"

Talk about stress! Within three weeks Pam Hetland had married, become an instant mother to her husband's nine-year-old son, moved to another city, and started a new job. That month her employer required all personnel to take a stress test that warned of a "serious illness after 300 points." Pam's score was 329.

Something had to give. Just about that time, her husband, Ron, started a new business and needed a secretary. One day after interviewing several candidates, he called Pam to say, "I've seen more cleavage today than I've ever seen." Then he quickly added, "I'm hiring Diane, a pastor's wife. At least she knows how to dress. She starts tomorrow."

The next evening he had a story to tell. Diane, or "Dinny" as everyone called her, had a good sense of humor. One of Ron's coworkers had played a trick on her by dialing Ron's line and pretending he was Ron's parole officer, calling to remind him of his two o'clock appointment. Dinny had calmly replied that she would pass the information along. It was only when the caller burst into laughter that Dinny knew it was a joke. Then she said, "Maybe I should have asked Ron for a résumé, instead of giving him mine!"

The anecdote provided a pleasant chuckle at dinner, and Pam said she was looking forward to meeting Dinny someday. But she promptly forgot her intentions as she juggled her new responsibilities and longed for her family and former coworkers, now 150 miles away. She was especially lonely for her women friends.

Late one afternoon as she tried to prepare dinner, supervise homework, and do the laundry, the thought hit her that she worked in an office with all men and lived with all men. As she picked up the laundry basket, she muttered, "I'm lonely for women to talk to."

Immediately the thought popped into her head, *Call Dinny.* She paused. *Dinny? Who in the world is Dinny?* she wondered. "Oh, Ron's secretary," she said aloud.

That night after dinner she took a deep breath and looked up Dinny's number. After exchanging the typical pleasantries, including how pleased she was that Dinny was working with Ron, Pam said, "I'd like to join a group where I can get to know some women. Do you have any suggestions?"

Dinny was delighted. "Oh, yes! I'm in an evening Bible study I really like," she said. "In fact, we're meeting tomorrow night. I'll be glad to swing by and pick you up."

A Bible study? Pam thought nervously. That wasn't exactly what she'd had in mind, but she was so desperate for companionship that she was willing to give it a try. Less than twenty-four hours later, Pam was sitting with Dinny and twenty-five other women when the leader asked the group to turn to Ephesians 3. Dinny, trying to be helpful as Pam thumbed awkwardly through the Scriptures, whispered, "It's right next to Galatians." Of course, that didn't do Pam any good because she didn't know where Galatians was either. But just being with other women was a boost to Pam's spirits.

Shortly after that first Bible study, Dinny invited Pam to lunch. As they talked about their backgrounds, Pam told Dinny about her move away from all that was familiar, then asked, "What do you do when you're lonely?"

Dinny smiled, "I pray a lot. With my husband being a pastor, he often gets called away, so I just lean on the Lord all the more."

Pam looked bewildered. "But how does someone you can't see help you?"

"Oh, it's true I can't see him," Dinny answered. "But I feel his presence, and I know he's helping me whenever I ask him. He isn't a bellboy who jumps to our every whim, but he's the God of the universe, the one who gave his Son to save us from our sins. John 3:16 comes to mind every time I pray."

Pam frowned. "John 3:16?"

Dinny nodded. "John 3:16 says, 'For God so loved the world that he gave his one and only Son, that whoever believes in him shall not perish but have eternal life.' Because of Jesus' death on the cross, we can go directly to the Father."

Dinny paused, then asked, "Pam, have you ever made a commitment to trust Jesus as your Lord and Savior?" When Pam shook her head, Dinny explained, "Trusting him is very simple—as easy as ABC, in fact. *Acknowledge* that you need him, *believe* that he died for your sins, and *commit* to live for him."

Pam leaned forward. "I'd like to do that." And right there, over lunch, Dinny led the young woman in her first prayer—and for salvation at that.

From there, friendship grew. Soon it was common for the two women to call each other in the middle of the day to ask for prayer about whatever was going on at the moment. Those phone calls became especially important because of a rocky relationship with Ron's son. Sometimes when Pam called Dinny with a concern, the older woman would say, "I'll pray that God will change Ron's heart on that." Other times she'd say, "Now Pam, I don't think you handled that very well."

Pam was comforted to know somebody was praying who had a little cooler head than Pam felt she had.

While wondering if her feelings would be different if the boy were her own son, Pam tuned into a radio ministry broadcast that Dinny had recommended. The day's guest was discussing blended families, a topic that immediately caught Pam's attention. She heard the guest speaker say, "I realized that I didn't have to love my stepchildren in the same way their mother did. But God did call me to do right by them."

That simple statement freed Pam. In that moment she understood that, while she might not be able to duplicate a natural parent's love for her stepson, she could reaffirm her commitment to him even while disapproving of his actions.

Once, as Pam tried to thank Dinny for all that she meant to her, Dinny insisted she wasn't special. "I'm not even a good pastor's wife because I don't know how to play the piano and I don't bake bread. All the other pastors' wives do those things!" she chuckled.

Pam shook her head. "But Dinny, I'd hate to think where I'd be if you hadn't come along."

Dinny hugged her. "Oh, that's God's grace. He didn't just give me to you; he gave *you* to *me*." Pam smiled and silently thanked God for giving her the notion to "call Dinny." Now Pam would never be the same.

Chapter Nineteen

Polishing Rainbows

Leah* glanced at the other couples in the Bible study group, wondering if any of them could tell that she and her husband were having trouble. *Trouble?* she thought. *Heading toward divorce is more like it.* There was no question that her husband wanted out of the marriage; he'd told her he hadn't signed on to deal with her "getting on his case" all the time. Leah grimaced. She didn't mean to nag; she just wanted things to go right.

Well, at least he was still here, if for no other reason than for the sake of their two children. And he was still in church and willing to attend this Bible study. Leah glanced at one of the women, Pam Carlson, chatting in the doorway with the pastor. She and her husband, a lovable teddy bear of a man, had moved to town recently. The pastor had asked Pam to give her testimony tonight. A few minutes later Pam stood before the group, pausing to look at each face before speaking.

---

* Not her real name

"I grew up in a non-Christian home," she began. "My family didn't have a Bible in the house. I never went to Sunday school. I was married at twenty to a man who had been raised in a wonderful Christian family and whose parents did not judge me but accepted me totally. Oh, occasionally on Sunday afternoons they would call to ask if we had gone to church—and occasionally we had—but church left me feeling empty inside. At the same time, I had a Christian employer who was loving around her church friends but manipulative and cruel to many who worked for her. I remember thinking, *If this is Christianity, then I don't want anything to do with it.* But almost as an afterthought, I would think, *If you're out there, God, if you're real, then please show me.*

"Just a few days later, a friend called to invite me to a Billy Graham crusade. I went out of curiosity, but the clear presentation of the gospel and how it is supposed to be lived got my attention. To my surprise, I accepted the Lord that night. The crusade counselor gave me a list of Bible studies in my area, and the next thing I knew, I was in one led by a woman who had a knack for teaching new Christians. For a year I couldn't wait to pick up my Bible each day, even though I still wasn't going to church.

"It wasn't long before my husband, Jerry, commented, 'The God I hear you talking about isn't the same God I grew up with.' Then he added, 'I don't think I'm a Christian.' We invited my Bible study leader over for dinner so Jerry could ask questions. He wound up accepting the Lord that night. A little while later we found a Bible-believing church and were baptized together.

"What an exciting time that was for us! I continued with Bible study and did all I could to learn and grow, and pretty soon I was leading Bible studies myself. But then suddenly, at thirty-eight, I was diagnosed with multiple sclerosis. The disease progressed so rapidly that within a few months I could barely walk without help, and I couldn't use my hands for more than a year, not even to brush my teeth. But my husband was just wonderful. He gently helped me, tying my shoes or buttoning a blouse. Prior to that time we'd been caught in a power struggle. Suddenly this macho man, who was used to telling people what to do, had to serve me. But as I saw the tender way he was there for me, my heart just melted. My illness actually restored our love for each other."

A power struggle, Leah thought. *Is that what's going on with me and Hans?** Suddenly Leah felt hopeful. If this thing had a name, maybe it had a solution.

Leah glanced at Pam's husband, who sat smiling at his wife. Leah couldn't imagine Jerry being the way Pam had described him. Now he was an outgoing, gentle man with a big heart for people.

* Not his real name

Leah turned her attention back to Pam, who continued, "Early in my illness, I'd been studying the Word to see what God said about disease. I decided that my healing totally depended on how much faith I had, so I concentrated on nothing but God's power to restore me. But I was losing ground fast and was going to need a wheelchair soon. My, how I fought that! I kept saying, 'I know God will heal.' But finally one day I said, 'Well, Lord, I've trusted and believed that you were going to heal me; now I'm just going to accept whatever you do. If I'm flat on my back in bed and if that's the best way I can serve you, then I'm willing.' In that moment I felt like Abraham sacrificing Isaac; I just gave up all my wishes.

"I truly was at peace, but in just a few days I began to notice more strength in my body, and I could open and close my fingers. Then I could raise my hand to brush my teeth. Within a few weeks, my body was restored to what it is now. The only sign of MS remaining is the partial numbness in my legs. I can't do strenuous work, but otherwise I lead a totally normal life.

"A major lesson I learned in all this is the importance of relationships—with God and your spouse. That's all you have when all else fails."

Leah leaned forward, fighting tears. *Lord, please show me how to do my part to mend our marriage,* she asked silently. Later she made a special effort to thank Pam for her encouraging talk.

Pam called Leah a few days later. "I was praying for you this morning," she said. "Then the Lord nudged me to call you to talk about your marriage. How's it going?"

Leah started to sob. Pam said gently, "Leah, I grew up with two alcoholic parents. I was an only child caught up in constant problems and crises. Often it seemed as though I was the parent. So I was set up, I think, to see life in terms of 'something needs to be done; let's do it.' That outlook was causing those early power struggles in my marriage. Whatever is going on in yours isn't hopeless."

As Leah continued to sniffle, Pam's voice softened even more. "Sit on the Lord's lap, Leah," she said. "Picture his face as you talk to him. He's had to do a lot of healing from my childhood. I didn't have a father I was close to, so I've had to let the Lord take that role too."

As the two women talked, often pausing while Leah sobbed, a friendship was budding. In the weeks ahead Pam helped Leah understand her desperate need to control and showed her how to loosen her demands on her husband. To Leah's amazement, the tension in her marriage eased, and Hans actually began to look forward to spending time with her.

For two years Pam continued her role as spiritual mentor to Leah before Pam and her husband moved again. Of course, Leah missed Pam after the move, but they continued their friendship over the phone.

One day Leah shared with Pam the joy she and her husband experienced when Nicholas, their seven-year-old son, prayed to ask Jesus to be his Savior. As Leah had leaned forward to kiss his forehead, the boy had asked, "What will we do in heaven, Mommy?"

"Well, God said we'll have jobs," Leah had replied. "So we won't just sit around on clouds."

Nicholas had smiled at that. "Know what, Mom?" he said. "I want my job to be polishing rainbows."

As Pam expressed her delight at Leah's news, Leah said, "You share in our son's sweet decision, Pam. If it hadn't been for you, I'd probably be a divorced mother by now. Your time here was God's gift to me—and to my family."

What Leah didn't know was that those two years of being under Pam's teaching were also preparation for a coming tragedy. Three weeks after that conversation, Leah and her family were attending a reunion on a ranch several miles from home. As Leah and her five-year-old daughter picnicked, Hans and Nicholas rode together on a normally gentle horse. Suddenly something startled the animal and he reared, slamming Nicholas to the ground. During the long drive to the hospital, Leah knew he was already with the Lord. And yet, even with the tears running down her cheeks, she was filled with peace.

The days following the tragedy were a blur of relatives and funeral arrangements and phone calls—especially from Pam. Amazingly, Leah and her husband were able to comfort one another, even in the midst of intense grief. Leah was convinced that if the tragedy had happened three years earlier, their marriage would not have been strong enough to survive it. But two years of being in the Word and under Pam's shepherding had opened the doors for deeper communication.

A couple of weeks after Nicholas's death, Leah, Hans, and their daughter stepped out onto their deck after a rainstorm. Suddenly the little girl exclaimed excitedly, "Look! A rainbow!"

They turned to look at an incredible *double* rainbow. Leah gasped at the shimmering colors, then turned to her husband. "Remember when Nicholas said he wanted to be a rainbow polisher in heaven?" she asked softly. Hans nodded. "Well, he did a wonderful job on that one, huh?" she added.

Hans put his arm around Leah's waist and pulled her close. They would get through this—together.

———

To Ponder:

Pam not only gave Leah insight into her marriage problems but modeled a solution just by sharing what God had done in her own life. She wasn't aware that she was equipping Leah to handle not only her present marriage challenges but the future loss of her beloved son.

Do you ever think, "I can't help anyone. Who would want to learn anything from me? I've made lots of mistakes"? It doesn't matter. If you're willing simply to share your journey, you may find God using you to help build a stronger foundation in another's life.

When All Is Said and Done

Ask yourself what you will care about when everything is on the line. . . .

Achievements and the promise of posthumous acclaim will bring some satisfaction, no doubt. But your highest priorities will be drawn from another source. When all is said and done and the books are closing on your life, I believe your treasures will lie much closer to home. Your most precious memories will focus on those you loved, those who loved you, and what you did together in the service of the Lord. Those are the basics. Nothing else will survive the scrutiny of time.[17]

—DR. JAMES DOBSON

HOSPITALITY

Keep on loving each other as brothers. Do not forget to entertain strangers, for by so doing some people have entertained angels without knowing it.

HEBREWS 13:1-2

The King will reply, "I tell you the truth, whatever you did for one of the least of these brothers of mine, you did for me."

MATTHEW 25:40

Be devoted to one another in brotherly love. Honor one another above yourselves. . . . Share with God's people who are in need. Practice hospitality.

Bless those who persecute you; bless and do not curse. Rejoice with those who rejoice; mourn with those who mourn. Live in harmony with one another. Do not be proud, but be willing to associate with people of low position. Do not be conceited.

ROMANS 12:10,13-16

Reaching Beyond Ourselves

My heart's desire is to find more opportunities to give myself away and teach my children the joy of service at the same time. One little problem: When?! A friend of mine once moaned, "There's just not enough of me to go around." Lots of us feel the same way and can't bear the thought of adding one more activity, one more to do item to our list, however worthy it may be.

For busy women like us, who don't know how we could manage the added role of volunteer, psychologist Virginia O'Leary offers a word of encouragement: "The more roles women have, the better off they are, and the less likely they are to be depressed or discouraged about their lives. When we have a lot to do, we complain that it's driving us crazy—but, in fact, it's what keeps us sane."

It's ironic that one of the best remedies for impending burnout is to give yourself away. To pick one time and place each week where you stretch out your hands for the pure joy of doing it.[18]

—LIZ CURTIS HIGGS

Chapter Twenty

More Than a Room

Thee Brock tried not to panic the evening her roommate announced she was taking a job out of state and would be moving within two weeks.

"Moving?" Thee gasped. "Well, I'm happy for you. But I confess I don't know what I'm going to do. After all, I can't afford to rent this place alone."

Her roommate nodded. "I know. I hated to tell you because of that," she said. "I was hoping this would wait until you decided whether you were going to move to Miami. But what would you think about asking Joan Maseroni if you could rent her studio apartment?"

Thee looked surprised. "Joan? She wouldn't know me from Adam. I can't ask her."

Her roommate persisted. "At least ask," she said. "Joan and her husband sometimes rent to people who are caught in a difficult place."

That evening Thee took a deep breath and called Joan. She told her briefly about her roommate's pending move, then said, "Uh . . . I understand that sometimes you rent your studio apartment." She thought of mentioning she was African-American, but Joan was already responding.

"Well, the room is available right now," she said. "When would you like to look at it?"

Thee was suddenly hopeful. "I can stop in after work tomorrow, if that's convenient," she suggested. Joan said it was, so the next evening a nervous Thee rang the bell. Soon the door was opened by a lovely, dark-haired, smiling woman who threw her arms around Thee as soon as Thee introduced herself. Thee was a little taken aback but also intrigued. She'd never had a white woman welcome her like that. Also, hugging just wasn't something she had experienced a lot while growing up; she wasn't as comfortable with it as she wanted to be.

As those thoughts raced through Thee's mind, Joan said, "Now, come right in. I'll show you the room." As Joan led the way down the steps, she said, "You'll have to excuse my moving so slowly. It takes me awhile to get down stairs anymore. I have something the doctors call 'fibromyalgia,' which causes a lot of pain in my muscles. It affects my sleep too, so I usually don't get to sleep until two or three in the morning. Don't worry, though," she chuckled, "I don't wander all over the house. I just get up and read my Bible or listen to my worship tapes."

Thee opened her mouth to express her sympathy, but Joan was on to another subject. "Your name is lovely but unusual," she said. "Does it have an interesting story to go along with it?"

Thee laughed. "Nothing dramatic," she replied. "My name is actually Theolyn, which is a blend of my mother's name, Evelyn, and my paternal grandmother's, Theola. When I was eight, I was visiting my grandmother and playing with the neighbor's daughter who couldn't say my name. She asked if she could call me 'Thee' instead, and the nickname stuck."

Joan smiled. "That's a great story," she said. "I'm always intrigued by the events that make us who we are. Don't you find people fascinating?"

Thee started to answer, but Joan opened a door and said, "Well, here we are. Do you think this will do?"

From the hallway Thee could see a large bedroom, adjoining sitting room, and private bathroom. What she thought would be merely a small bedroom was actually a little apartment, clean and spacious. "Wow, this is great!" Thee said.

"So what do you think I should charge you?" Joan asked.

Thee was afraid to offer the little she could afford, but looking into Joan's kind eyes, she dared to say, "How about $150 a month?"—an incredibly low rate for that East Coast area.

Joan nodded, then said, "Well, let me ask my husband. He's in his study. You're welcome to look around."

Thee timidly did exactly that, almost holding her breath as she saw the space she might have. Within a few minutes Joan was back. "He agreed," she said. "When can you move in?" And just that easily, Thee had a new home—and a new friend.

In the months that followed, Thee had repeated opportunities to bask in Joan's kindness, love for people and the Lord, and ongoing encouragement. One evening, as Thee prepared to attend a work-related reception, Joan commented, "Thee, you're drop-dead gorgeous."

Thee laughed. "Joan, you're so prejudiced!"

Joan looked startled. "Prejudiced?" she repeated. The shocked look on Joan's face made Thee laugh all the harder.

"Yes, prejudiced! You never see anything wrong with me."

Joan smiled. "Well, you *are* drop-dead gorgeous."

On the way to the reception, Thee smiled again as she thought of the scene that was so characteristic of Joan. After just these few months, Thee was convinced she had become more confident, even outgoing, because of Joan's acceptance and encouragement. *What a treat to have a role model and a friend all in one,* she thought. Joan even influenced Thee's reactions to people; when she would have an inclination to be less than kind to somebody, she'd think of how Joan would respond.

Thee gripped the steering wheel with new excitement. *Maybe I'll even apply for that Miami job*, she thought. And she'd look into being a Big Sister to a child. In fact, she'd ask for the toughest case, someone who hadn't received much encouragement in life. Thee suddenly smiled. Maybe, just maybe, she'd even learn how to give Joan-sized hugs.

Chapter Twenty-One

An Important Invitation

When Judy Bannister's friends from church invited her to a singles' retreat, she didn't have to think twice. She had gone through a divorce recently and was anxious to begin healing emotionally; she thought that listening to speakers with practical points would help. She didn't know, however, that she'd be given an opportunity to ease her own hurts through being kind to another woman.

After a pleasant drive Judy and her friends arrived at the camp and headed for their cabin, which contained several bunk beds. The retreat receptionist had instructed them to choose their beds, unpack, and then go to the main conference area for the opening session. So after dumping their totes onto the nearest bunks, they prepared to head up the hill.

As they turned to go, Judy noticed a woman in the far corner—alone. Everyone else in the cabin had a friend or two with whom they were talking and laughing. If Judy had been alone, she would have hoped for someone to include her, so she called to the woman, "Come with us! We're going to the first session."

The woman smiled, closed her suitcase, and hurried to join Judy and her friends. As they walked together, Judy introduced herself, then discovered the woman's name was Fran and that she too had recently been divorced. She now was attending church for the first time in her life.

"I'm amazed you came to the retreat alone," Judy said. "I'm not that brave."

Fran managed a wry smile. "Oh, being brave had nothing to do with it," she said. "I had planned to come with another woman from church, but at the last minute she wasn't available after all. I knew I had to be here though."

As Judy asked more questions, Fran hesitantly began to talk about her divorce, especially the broken dreams. Soon she was crying, and she cried all through the service even though the speaker was amusing. Judy remembered her own endless tears and raw wounds. In fact, she wasn't that far away from them herself. Judy pulled a fresh tissue out of her purse and handed it to Fran.

As the program ended and the others headed to the snack shop, Judy and Fran walked slowly back to the cabin, still talking. This time Judy shared her story. For the rest of the weekend, the new friends went to meals together and attended every session in order to be reminded of God's love and to hear practical suggestions on how to cope with daily challenges.

On the last morning of the retreat, the host announced that in the final session they would have communion, which would be served in small groups. That's when Fran popped her life-changing question. "What is communion?" she asked Judy.

Communion was so basic to Judy that she was surprised by the question, but she explained simply, "Well, communion is a reminder that Jesus, the Son of God, died for us. We drink grape juice out of little cups—some churches use wine—and we break off little pieces of bread from a loaf. The juice symbolizes the blood that Jesus shed for us. The bread symbolizes his body. After he was buried, he rose from the grave on the third day, letting us know he overcame death and has provided eternal life for us."

Fran listened intently as Judy continued. "If we confess our sins and claim Jesus Christ as our Savior, we can participate in the communion service as a symbol of our faith," Judy explained. "If you decide you aren't ready for communion yet, that's okay. There will probably be others who won't participate, so don't feel embarrassed if you don't."

Fran nodded. "You mean that's it? All I have to do is believe that Jesus died for me?"

Judy smiled. "Salvation itself is simple. It's *living* the Christian life that gets a little challenging at times. But this is how the new life begins."

Fran looked thoughtful. "I need to think about

this. I can't take part in something I don't believe, but I know I need his help. And I have a lot of things to talk to him about." Fran went off for a walk by herself, saying she'd meet Judy before the next session. During that service Judy noticed that Fran not only took the elements but treated them like sacred items.

As Judy and Fran prepared to leave the conference that afternoon, they exchanged phone numbers and made plans to get together the following week. Soon Judy invited Fran to visit her church. During the first Sunday school class, the social committee passed around a sign-up sheet for the Christmas party, which Fran immediately signed. Judy was surprised to see Fran jumping in so quickly but was pleased she felt welcome.

Little did either of them know that a particular gentleman in the class had noticed Fran as soon as she walked through the door. Not long after the Christmas party, it was evident that he was very interested in her. Gradually they began to see each other regularly. Six months later they married, crediting Judy with introducing them.

In Judy's eyes, that "chance" meeting at a weekend retreat has been one of the greatest blessings God has ever given her. Looking back, she thinks about how little effort was required simply to befriend a lonely woman. But, oh, the eternal benefits of that first kind word!

To Ponder:

A simple greeting and friendly welcome led to a drastic change in Fran's life. No special skills were required of Judy, no special personality—just the act of reaching out and saying, "Come join us." Yet through that simple gesture, a new soul was brought into God's kingdom.

Consider your activities. Can you include someone new? You never know when a simple greeting might become the most important invitation in someone's life!

From the Heart

Mend a quarrel.

Search out a forgotten friend.

Dismiss a suspicion and replace it with a trust.

Write a letter to someone who misses you.

Encourage a youth who has lost his faith.

Keep a promise.

Forget an old grudge.

Examine your demands on others.

Fight for a principle.

Express your gratitude.

Overcome an old fear.

Take time to appreciate the beauty of nature.

Give God the praise.

Tell someone you love them.

Tell them again, and again, and again.[19]

—AUTHOR UNKNOWN

Chapter Twenty-Two

A Place to Heal

Pat Bigliardi laughed appreciatively as the Vietnamese waiter kidded about American stomachs not being up to his homeland's spicy dishes. But the group visiting the ministry where she worked part-time had really wanted to go to this restaurant. *Besides,* Pat thought, *I'm Italian. I can handle anything.*

The lunch meeting went well, but when Pat stood up, she felt a strange constriction in her left arm, as though someone was starting to pump a blood pressure cup. She flexed and unflexed her fingers and then gave her shoulders a slight roll. Boy, that food must have hit her faster than she expected.

When she got out onto the street with the rest of the group, the tightness in her arm seemed to increase. *What if it wasn't the food?* she thought. *Lord, please don't let me have a heart attack here on the street,* she prayed half-jokingly. She immediately dismissed the thought. She was only forty-one. It had to be the food.

For the rest of the day, Pat moved slowly. Her schedule had been rather intense lately; maybe she just needed to catch her breath. Just a couple of days before, she had moved into the home of a fellow single mother from church. The living arrangements would help both women financially. Pat planned to move her teenage son's things over to the new place this coming weekend.

That night Pat went to bed early. She had a fitful night, however, and she still didn't feel well the next morning, so she took the day off. As she rested throughout the day, she was aware of other aggravations. It began to feel as though she had a pinched nerve in her back—probably from that car accident years ago. As the day wore on, the pinched nerve got a little tighter. Maybe she at least ought to call her doctor friend from church.

"Do you have chest pain?" was his first question.

"No. Just this weird pinched nerve that's affecting my arm, too," Pat answered.

"Any nausea?" he asked.

"No," Pat said. "Yesterday I ate some spicy food, and it's still sitting a little heavy in my stomach, but that's all."

"Well, just rest today," the doctor said. "But call me if you get chest pain."

By evening she still had no chest pain, but Pat sat up all night in discomfort since lying down made her short of breath. The next morning she was moving very slowly, and her lungs felt as though they weren't fully inflating. Maybe she ought to stop by the hospital on her way to work. She'd feel silly when the doctors patted her on the head and sent her home, but at least she'd know it was nothing serious.

By the time Pat arrived at the emergency room, her breathing had become labored and her back was hurting even more. When Pat described the symptoms to the emergency room receptionist, a nurse quickly appeared, gave her nitroglycerin, and ushered her into a cubicle. The attending physician said that as a precaution they'd do an electrocardiogram. So Pat lay quietly on the gurney, waiting for the nitro to take effect. Her heart seemed to have settled down.

After reading the EKG, a doctor and nurse came in. "Mrs. Bigliardi, it was good that you decided to come in when you did," the doctor said. "Don't be alarmed; we're right here, but you're in the midst of a heart attack right now."

As Pat gasped, the nurse patted her shoulder. The doctor murmured reassuringly, "We're here. You're okay."

Immediately Pat underwent medical tests, including a echocardiogram, which showed a clot that had caused her heart to go into spasms during the previous two days. The doctors decided to do what was then a new procedure: They'd run a catheter from her groin up into the heart and insert medicine right into the clot to dissolve it. Her new housemate, Janice, had already activated the prayer chain, so Pat knew her church was praying.

Pat was in the hospital ten days. What she didn't know during her recovery, however, was that Janice was dealing with her own stress. The morning before Pat was supposed to go home, Janice had gone to an elder and said, "I don't think I can handle this. I have four young children, and I don't know how to take care of someone recovering from a heart attack. I have to work, so I can't be available. I don't know what to do."

The elder had quickly assured her that, of course, she couldn't be expected to take care of Pat. "She can't move in with you," he responded immediately. Then he offered to tell Pat himself.

That evening he went to the hospital and told Pat as gently as possible, "Janice is stressed by all of this. She can't take care of you when she has four young children and a demanding job. This is not a good situation. It would be better if you found another place to live."

Pat merely nodded and said, "Okay." The elder offered a quick prayer and left. Pat's head was reeling with the news. Where was she going to live? Her nearest relative, a very pregnant sister, was five hundred miles away.

In that moment, Pat's doctor came in with what

he thought was good news: She was doing so well, he was going to release her the first thing the next day. Reality hit. "But I don't have a place to live!" Pat wailed. Adding trauma to her situation was exactly what the doctor didn't want to do, so he offered quick assurance that she could stay a few more days.

As the doctor closed the door behind him, Pat began to sob. "God, this is it," she prayed aloud as tears ran down her cheeks. "I have nothing. No insurance. No home. I don't even have enough money to check into a hotel. Kelly can live with his dad for a while, but where am I going? God, help me. You're it. There are no human resources for me."

Exhausted, Pat sank into her pillows, her arm covering her eyes. When the phone on the bedside table rang, she was tempted to ignore it, but she finally picked it up, thinking it might be her son. No, just Martha, a friend who was in the process of moving.

"How ya doing?" Martha asked.

Pat rubbed her eyes to clear the tears. "Awful!" she answered. "The doctor was just in to tell me I can go home tomorrow, but I don't have a place to live! Janice is stressed over the thought of having me come back there. I don't know what I'm going to do."

Martha sighed sympathetically, then said, "Listen, Pat, the kids and I will pray. And I'll call Mom and Dad and ask them to pray too."

Pat managed a wan smile. Martha's parents, Dorothy and Leo Ruth, were dear people. *If they're praying, everything is going to be all right,* Pat thought. She had met the Ruths eight years earlier at the condominium complex where she'd lived just after she'd become a Christian. Dorothy's quick smile had won Pat over immediately, so when Dorothy had invited Pat to a Bible study, Pat had quickly accepted even though she didn't know what to expect. Now even thinking of the woman with the beautiful silver hair and deep blue eyes calmed Pat.

As soon as Martha hung up the phone, she called her parents to explain Pat's plight. "The Lord already has provided a place," Dorothy said. "Pat is going to stay with us for two months. After your dad having that heart attack last year, I certainly know how to take care of someone who's recovering from one. What's her number? I'll call her right now and invite her."

Within a few minutes, Dorothy Ruth was saying to Pat, "Would you consider coming to live with us for two months here at the beach? We'd love to have you recuperate with us. I can pick you up."

Pat almost squealed with delight. The Ruths' new home was on the water. What a perfect spot for recovery!

The next morning, after a pleasant drive, Pat was further cheered by Dorothy and Leo's assuring her,

"Nothing is required of you here but to get well." For the next two months, Pat concentrated on doing just that. She rested, awakened to ocean sounds, and walked the secluded beach. Dorothy took Pat to the grocery store and bought only what Pat could eat. They even invited Pat's son and friends down for weekends so she wouldn't feel lonely. And each day she and Dorothy studied the Bible together.

Gradually Pat realized that this peaceful time was good not only for her physical heart but for her spiritual heart as well. Studying the Word and talking over each passage with Dorothy helped Pat build a stronger spiritual foundation. Occasionally Pat shed tears of thanksgiving as she mended under Dorothy's watchful care.

One afternoon while walking on the beach, Pat waved to Dorothy and Leo as they sipped tea on the deck. Dorothy waved back and gestured for Pat to join them. Pat headed eagerly up the stairs, feeling her heart pump solidly within.

To Ponder:
When Dorothy opened her home, she did more than just solve Pat's need for a place to live; she gave a part of herself that helped Pat feel confident again about her future. Dorothy probably didn't realize the emotional and spiritual

healing that her hospitality contained as she simply shared her heart and her space with another woman.

When you offer even a simple act of hospitality, perhaps it too will have a much bigger impact on someone's life than you would ever dream.

For God's Pleasure

"Now it happened one day that Elisha went to Shunem, where there was a notable woman, and she constrained him to eat some food. So it was, as often as he passed by, that he turned in there to eat some food. And she said to her husband, 'Look now, I know that this is a holy man of God, who passes by us regularly. Please, let us make a small upper room on the wall; and let us put a bed for him there, and a table and a chair and a lampstand; so it will be, whenever he comes to us, he can turn in there'" (2 Kings 4:8-10).

Some people have the gift of hospitality. This well-to-do woman from Shunem was one of them. She used her means to bless and refresh others. She had discerned that Elisha was God's prophet, but she also knew that he was hungry and tired. She and her husband anticipated his needs for rest, reflection, and reading. They gave the best they had, and God rewarded them by giving this childless couple a son. God rewarded her hospitality to His prophet with the desire of her heart.

When was the last time you were refreshed by the hospitality of one of God's thoughtful children? Refresh someone soon with a body and soul stopover at your expense and for God's pleasure.[20]

—JAN CARLBERG

GODLINESS

The wise in heart are called discerning,
  and pleasant words promote instruction.

PROVERBS 16:21

Remain in me, and I will remain in you. No branch can bear fruit by itself; it must remain in the vine. Neither can you bear fruit unless you remain in me.

I am the vine; you are the branches. If a man remains in me and I in him, he will bear much fruit; apart from me you can do nothing.

JOHN 15:4-5

Finally, brothers, whatever is true, whatever is noble, whatever is right, whatever is pure, whatever is lovely, whatever is admirable—if anything is excellent or praiseworthy—think about such things. Whatever you have learned or received or heard from me, or seen in me—put it into practice. And the God of peace will be with you.

PHILIPPIANS 4:8-9

Sweet Fragrance

The story has been told of a missionary to China who was in language school. The very first day of class the teacher entered the room and, without saying a word, walked down every row of students. Finally, still without saying a word, she walked out of the room again. Then she came back and addressed the class.

"Did you notice anything special about me?" she asked. Nobody could think of anything in particular. One student finally raised her hand. "I noticed that you had on a very lovely perfume," she said. The class chuckled. But the teacher said, "That was exactly the point. You see, it will be a long time before any of you will be able to speak Chinese well enough to share the Gospel with anyone in China. But even before you are able to do that, you can minister the sweet fragrance of Christ to these people by the quality of your lives. It is your lifestyle, lived out among the Chinese people, that will minister Christ to them long before you are able to say one word to them about personal faith in Jesus."[21]

—MICHAEL P. GREEN

Chapter Twenty-Three

Spring of Faith

During the summer of 1944, drought caused wells in Harlan County, Kentucky, to dry up. Purchasing water for more than drinking was too expensive, so when clothes needed to be washed, Nancy Farley did like others in her little community—she carried river water up a steep bank from the sluggish Cumberland River. She then poured the muddy water through several layers of thin cloth in a futile attempt to strain it.

Nancy also carried water for the flowers her mother-in-law, Mintie, grew in a narrow strip of soil between the river and the road. The flowers were the one pleasure Mintie allowed herself, and she justified their existence by occasionally offering bouquets for sale to travelers.

The drought had taken all but the strongest plants, and those were kept alive by the scant dipperful of dirty river water that Mintie poured over them, grumbling all the while. Nancy would gently try to remind Mintie that the Lord would send water in his time, but Mintie usually responded to such statements from her daughter-in-law with silence. One afternoon she gave an exasperated snort, then said, "Are you telling me he's interested in getting us water? I wouldn't count on that if I were you."

Nancy wasn't one to let her faith be challenged without an answer. "Now, I don't know how he's going to help us, but he will. Maybe it will be as simple as keeping us strong enough to lug the water up the river-bank. Or maybe, when he's through teaching us more about faith and patience, he'll give us a good rain shower."

Mintie searched the cloudless blue sky above the mountains and snorted again. "Why don't you just ask for a spring of water to bubble up from the dry ground? You're as likely to get the one as the other." Then she turned and went back into the house.

Nancy's brick home was well-built, but it had revealed one flaw when heavy rains fell shortly after its construction a decade before. A leak appeared in the corner of the basement. Nancy's husband, Carter, who built the house with their sons, dug a basin in the floor to contain the water. Then the leak disappeared just as strangely as it had begun, and the basin—roughly three feet wide and five feet long—remained dry thereafter.

After one particularly tiring day of lugging water for laundry up the riverbank, Nancy stretched out on the sofa, her very sighs a prayer for water. Almost immediately she jumped up off the sofa and called for her youngest daughter.

"Come with me, honey! The Lord just showed me the prettiest stream of water flowing from under my head. He's got water for us!"

Before her daughter could catch up with her, Nancy had grabbed a chisel and headed for the basement. Without hesitation she began to chop at the clay in the bottom of the corner basin.

"The sofa is right over this spot," she told her daughter excitedly. "I know the water's here."

When several minutes of enthusiastic digging produced nothing, Nancy prayed aloud. "Now, Lord, you showed me the water. Help me hit it this time."

Suddenly the clay grew dark around the chisel, and soon clear, fresh spring water bubbled up over the spot. Nancy quickly stepped out of the basin to keep her feet from getting wet, all the while exclaiming, "Thank you, Lord!" as she grabbed her daughter in a joyous hug.

Mintie heard the commotion and came grumbling down the steps. When she saw the basin filling with fresh, clean water, she was speechless. Nancy called her to come closer. "Look, Mintie! The Lord gave us water! And there'll be plenty for your flowers. You'll never have to pour muddy river water over them again!"

By then Mintie had found her voice. "What are you saying? You think just because there's a bit of water today that it's going to be there forever? That'll be all seeped out by morning."

Nancy never stopped smiling. "Oh, no, it won't! The Lord gave it, and he won't let it run out for as long as this family needs it. And to think it was here all the time, just waiting for us. Oh, God is so good. He always provides."

She was right. Mintie never had to use river water again on her flowers. Not only did the spring supply water for her family, but there was enough for all the neighbors in that little community too. Nancy refused to be stingy with what the Lord had given, and the spring never went dry as long as a member of her extended family owned the house.

Because of Nancy's faith, Mintie gained a new respect for the Lord—and for Nancy. She no longer made sarcastic remarks about her daughter-in-law's beliefs and even began joining the family for their evening devotions. And she insisted upon telling any dinner visitor all about the origin of the cool, sweet water that was served with every meal—the water released by one woman's faith.

To Ponder:

Nancy's faith helped her look beyond obvious challenges to the Lord's miraculous solutions. And in the process, her mother-in-law's cynicism was disrupted.

Have you been affected by the faith of another woman? Do you ever wonder what "springs" within your own life are waiting to be released by your faith?

Chapter Twenty-Four

Another View of Jesus

Laura Hufford thumbed through her Bible, waiting for her husband to join her in the third row of the chapel at the church camp where they were vacationing. She had so hoped the week would jump-start her spiritual sensitivities, but here it was the fourth day, and she was still aware of a quiet frustration that seemed to sit just below the surface. Her life was, well, sometimes a little too calm. Oh, she certainly didn't want anything tragic to happen to shake things up, but she needed a challenge. The children were older now and not so demanding. She sighed. *Oh, well. Maybe tonight's speaker will be interesting,* she thought hopefully.

Just then Laura became aware of commotion behind her. As she turned, she saw a couple directing a group of children down the aisle—all of them disabled in one way or another. The woman, just a little older than Laura, had a patient, loving expression as she guided two children carrying white canes to the front row.

Laura quickly counted the woman's charges. One, two, three . . . wow! *Nine* children, ranging in age from about four to fourteen, filled the front row. In addition to the two blind youngsters were two Down syndrome children, one girl in a wheelchair, little ones wearing protective helmets, one on metal crutches, and a deaf boy about eleven who watched the woman closely. As she gestured for him to sit on the far end of the pew, he gave her a quick smile and settled in for the service.

Laura couldn't keep her eyes off the children. They were so well-behaved, the older ones watching out for the younger ones. When her husband joined her and Laura motioned toward the group, he too watched, fascinated.

During the service the group was called to the front, where the woman, Karen Watts, told about their unusual family. Laura found her eyes filling with tears as Karen described each child, all abandoned by mothers who couldn't cope with a disabled child. One of the blind children had been a crack baby and had needed to be held for days as he howled through withdrawal.

Laura, a teacher, was stunned by the accounts. *I'm good with kids,* she thought. *But this woman is phenomenal to handle all these situations and love these kids unconditionally.*

Laura and her husband, Larry, glanced at each other as Karen mentioned the need for financial sponsors.

After the service, as Karen and her husband, Ralph, helped the children into the van, Laura whispered to Karen that she and Larry had decided to help support them each month.

Early the next week Laura finished the vacation laundry, then called Karen to ask if she could help prepare dinner one evening. Karen immediately accepted. Two nights later, as they peeled a sack of potatoes together, Laura said, "You and Ralph are incredible."

Karen laughed. "Believe me, we're not."

"Well, how did you wind up doing this?" Laura asked.

"We were the typical American couple, trying to fill our hearts with *things*," Karen answered. "We had a comfortable lifestyle, but we knew there had to be more to life than just collecting stuff. We were meant to help children. Our own children were grown, so we wanted to move where we could do the most good."

Laura glanced out the kitchen window of the restored Victorian house in a run-down neighborhood. "But here?" she asked.

"We're certainly not saying everybody has to move to the inner city," Karen answered. "The point is to serve the Lord wherever he places you. He's placed us here—and he's given us these special children."

Karen continued. "Colossians 1:10 helped us make our decision. It says, 'And we pray this in order that you may live a life worthy of the Lord and may please him in every way: bearing fruit in every good work, growing in the knowledge of God.' We knew a life that centered on material possessions wasn't a life worthy of the Lord, so we started asking him to use our love for children and our desire to reach out to the inner city. Soon after, we heard about a child with special needs. Then we heard about another . . . and another."

"But why did you decide to help children with so many needs?" Laura persisted.

"Well, the 'perfect' children weren't having problems being placed," Karen answered. "We wanted to help children who didn't have a place waiting. And as far as their 'needs' go, when you love them along with taking care of them, their needs really aren't burdensome; they're just an extra challenge."

Laura reached for another potato. "But how do you keep everything running so smoothly?" she asked.

Karen smiled. "Oh, this house runs on prayer. Another necessity is order. 'A place for everything and everything in its place.' Not in an obsessive way, but just so we know where everything is."

Laura lowered her voice. "But doesn't all this put stress on your marriage?"

Karen laughed. "On the contrary; our marriage is thriving. Ralph and I both feel more fulfilled when we're serving and helping others."

Laura confided, "I'm trying to learn that when

God tells me to do something, I'm going to be happiest if I go ahead and do it. But I have a tendency to 'discuss' it with him. Sometimes I even go at it tooth and nail and tell him, 'God, I'm not going to do that.'"

Karen nodded with understanding, then suggested, "But he's not going to ask you to do anything he hasn't gifted you for."

Suddenly Laura remembered the stacked canned goods she had seen on the front porch. She asked about them.

"Oh, one of the men at church owns a grocery store," Karen answered. "He passes along the dented goods to us, so we leave them for neighbors, no questions asked."

That night Laura shared the details of this conversation with her husband. "I'd like to get to know them more," Laura said. "Do you think maybe we could help them out one weekend a month?"

Larry smiled. "Sure. I'd like that too."

And that's how Laura and Larry found themselves at the Watts home two weeks later, being awakened a little after midnight by the sound of police helicopters. As Laura looked out the window, she saw a SWAT team in the neighboring backyard, calling out drug dealers. As she burrowed back under the covers, she had to smile. *Well,* Laura admitted to herself, *I certainly can no longer complain about leading a boring life.*

To Ponder:

Laura says that watching Karen gave her another view of Jesus. "I can see him in the Scripture, but she is someone I can see here on earth," Laura explained.

God may not call you to live in the inner city or take care of numerous needy children, but as you respond to his leading and accept the responsibilities he brings your way, you just may provide another view of Jesus to someone else.

"Is Your God Like You?"

Jim, an elder at a church, was to oversee the evangelism of new people that moved into the area. Sun Lee and his family were Vietnamese refugees who had recently moved into the area. They had no possessions, knew no one, and needed help in every way. Jim began by helping them to get food and then spent much time finding Sun Lee a good job. Jim wanted so much to tell Sun Lee about Jesus Christ, but he didn't know Vietnamese and the refugees knew very little English. Both men sought to learn the other's language so that they could become better friends.

One day, Jim felt he knew enough now to tell Sun Lee about Jesus. Jim began to explain about God and Jesus to Sun Lee, but the more he talked, the more confusing it seemed to get. Sun Lee would repeat in Vietnamese a little of what Jim said in English. Finally, Jim was so frustrated that he decided to give up trying to communicate until he had learned more Vietnamese. Sun Lee at this point blurted out, "Is your God like you? If He is, I want to know Him."

Jim explained that Jesus Christ was greater than he was, far greater. Yet Sun Lee wanted to know more about Jesus Christ if He was like Jim! Jim had thought for all these months that he was not communicating the Gospel. But he was, with the greatest form of communication a person can use—the example of a life filled with Jesus Christ.

How are you at communicating the Gospel of Christ, both verbally and nonverbally? In order to distribute His fragrance effectively you need to be fragrantly spilled out in both respects.[22]

—MICHAEL P. GREEN AND SANDY PETRO

Chapter Twenty-Five

God's Beautiful Woman

Claudia Lind watched the rain beat against the back window. She was thankful she hadn't planned anything for the day other than cleaning out the upstairs closet and getting organized for the start of her children's new school year.

Within a few minutes she was elbow deep in last winter's mittens and gloves, games with missing pieces, and boxes of family photos. Then from the back of the closet, she pulled out a covered box labeled "Fun Stuff" in her mother's handwriting. Still on her knees, she opened it, then gave an "ah" of recognition. She'd forgotten that her mother had sent these papers. They were Claudia's drawings, report cards, and short stories from elementary school. And what was this? A certificate from vacation Bible school, signed by Helen Teagarden.

Suddenly Claudia was transported back to that little country Sunday school that Helen and her husband, Jerry, had started for the community. There was no church in the area, so Helen had thought, *Well, at least we can have a Sunday school.* The Teagardens purchased a small piece of property that had a chapel on it. Then they bought a little bus and became missionaries to the children in the area, collecting them each Sunday morning.

Claudia's brother, who was only five when Helen and Jerry moved into the area, was the first on their street to ride the little bus. He told so many stories about the interesting things he was learning each week that it wasn't long before Claudia's entire family, along with several other people from the area, were attending the little Sunday school in the middle of nowhere.

Claudia's brow wrinkled in thought as she recalled how Jerry had died just a few years after they'd started the Sunday school. But even after his death Helen never missed a beat. She was there Sunday after Sunday, supplying the materials, overseeing vacation Bible school, recruiting teachers. Every Christmas she put on a program, and any child old enough to talk was encouraged to take part. Claudia chuckled as she thought of one little girl who in her nervousness began to roll her dress in her hands. Soon she had rolled the dress up over her head—but she didn't stop reciting her poem.

When Claudia was about twelve, she wanted to help teach the younger children. One day she asked Helen about it. The older woman put an arm around her and said, "I'd love to have you as my helper, honey. You can tell the flannel-graph story." Claudia was thrilled with the responsibility.

It was in that little chapel that Claudia's brother and sister and Claudia herself all received the Lord as Savior because Helen presented the gospel in a simple and clear manner. It was there that Claudia's mother prayed publicly for the first time. There couldn't have been twenty people present that morning, but she had been scared to death. Helen hugged her afterward and told her it was a beautiful prayer.

Claudia leaned against the wall, lost in memories of Helen's encouragement and the love that drew people not only to her but to the Lord. They all had grown as believers under her care in the little Sunday school that became a light in their community.

Once, when she was a young teen, Claudia overheard a woman describe Helen as a *beautiful* lady. Claudia was astounded. To her, Helen had always appeared *round*. Helen's body was round; her face was round; her glasses were thick and round. She was just *round*. To a teen, that did not constitute beauty. But now, as Claudia held the certificate, she whispered, "Yes, beautiful. I bet that's just how Jesus sees her."

Claudia gently put the certificate back into the box. *We'll never see Helen Teagarden's name in lights,* she thought. *She never led a crusade or sang at a concert, but*

I'll bet she's got a jewel in her crown. And if the crown has a label, that label is Faithful Servant.

"Thank you, Helen," Claudia whispered. "You were indeed a beautiful woman."

In the Company of Roses

Roses are grown for the Vienna market in great profusion and with much distillation of fragrance. We are told that if you were to visit that valley at the time of the rose crop, wherever you would go the rest of the day, the fragrance you would carry with you would betray where you had been.

There is a beautiful parable given to us by the Persian poet and moralist, Saadi. The poet was given a bit of ordinary clay. The clay was so redolent with sweet perfume that its fragrance filled all the room.

"What are you, musk or ambergris?" he questioned.

"I am neither," it answered. "I am just a bit of common clay."

"From where then do you have this rare perfume?" the poet asked.

"I have companied all the summer with a rose," it replied.

We are just bits of the common clay of humanity. But if we company with the One who is the Rose of Sharon . . . something of the fragrance of His life will pass into ours. Then we will be a freshening and a sweetening influence to the world around us.[23]

—HENRY GARIEPY

The Heart's Cry

Dear Lord,

How I long to be what you would have me to be. How I thirst after a way to pour myself out for you like the fragrance of the incense Mary poured upon your head and feet. I want to share your love that fills my heart—to let others see and feel your loving touch as I do.

Father, I would love to be a vessel, however imperfect, that you could use to pour yourself out to others.

Lord, I would like to lift my voice and sing a beautiful song about you . . . or write a book that would change people's lives as they read of you and your love and care . . . or go to the inner city or a developing country and preach and teach and lay a cool healing hand on the heads of your sick and wounded and lost children.

Lord, I want to serve you. But how can I? I'm not gifted at preaching or teaching or singing or writing. But how I would love to be your hand to touch someone, Lord . . . to make a real difference in another's life just because you and I are there together.

Please show me how, Lord. Please use me. Please bless someone through me. Love through me, weep through me, speak through me.

Amen.

—BOBBIE VALENTINE

Notes

1. Stephen Hopper, "Onesiphorus: A Refresher Course," *Discipleship Journal* 35 (1986): 6, quoted in David Jeremiah, *Acts of Love* (Gresham, Ore.: Vision House, 1994), 57. Used by permission.

2. Author unknown, quoted in Jeremiah, *Acts of Love*, 87.

3. Vickie Kraft, *The Influential Woman* (Nashville: Word, 1992), 182-3. Reprinted with permission. All rights reserved.

4. Donna Partow, *Becoming a Vessel God Can Use* (Minneapolis: Bethany, 1996), 15. Reprinted with permission. All rights reserved.

5. Catherine Marshall, *Meeting God at Every Turn* (Grand Rapids: Chosen Books, 1980), 134-5, quoted in Judith Couchman, *Designing a Woman's Life* (Sisters, Ore.: Multnomah, 1995), 23.

6. Edith Schaeffer, *The Tapestry* (Waco: Word, 1981), 421.

7. John Duckworth, *Just for a Moment I Saw the Light* (Colorado Springs, Colo.: Victor Books, 1994), 217-8. Reprinted with permission. All rights reserved.

8. Margaret Cooke with Elizabeth Putman, *Ways You Can Help* (New York: Warner Books, 1996), 1-2.

9. Saint Paul's Evangelical Lutheran Church,

Sassamansville, Pa., quoted in Partow, *Becoming a Vessel*, 197-8.

10. Paul Borthwick, "Sink or Swim: Your Ministry of Encouragement," *Discipleship Journal* 54 (November-December 1981): 10, quoted in Jeremiah, *Acts of Love,* 87.

11. Joseph Bayly, *The Last Thing We Talk About* (London: Scripture Union, 1973), 40-1.

12. Claire Cloninger, *When God Shines Through* (Dallas: Word, 1988, 1994), as quoted in Terri A. Gibbs, ed., *Joy for the Journey* (Nashville: Word, 1997), 132.

13. Kraft, *The Influential Woman*, 146.

14. Elisabeth Elliot, *The Shaping of a Christian Family* (Nashville: Nelson, 1992), 157 as quoted in Gibbs, *Joy for the Journey,* 14. Reprinted with permission.

15. Paul Borthwick, *Six Dangerous Questions to Transform Your View of the World* (Downers Grove, Ill.: InterVarsity Press, 1996), 97-101. Used by permission of InterVarsity Press, P.O. Box 1400, Downers Grove, IL 60515.

16. Brad Humphrey with Teresa Vining, from a publisher's catalog describing *This Thing Called Christianity* (Chicago: Moody Press, 1996).

17. James Dobson, *Life on the Edge* (Dallas: Word, 1995), 268. Reprinted with permission. All rights reserved.

18. Liz Curtis Higgs, *Only Angels Can Wing It* (Nashville: Nelson, 1995), 127. Reprinted with permission.

19. Author unknown, quoted in June Hunt, *God's Heart on Encouragement,* Box 7, Dallas, TX 75221.

20. Jan Carlberg, *The Hungry Heart* (Brentwood, Tenn.: Wolgemuth & Hyatt, 1991), as quoted in Gibbs, *Joy for the Journey,* 24.

21. Michael P. Green, *Illustrations for Biblical Preaching* (Grand Rapids, Mich.: Baker, 1989), 77, quoted in Sandy Petro, *Discover Your Gift of Fragrance* (Colorado Springs, Colo.: Victor Books, 1991), 99. Reprinted with permission.

22. Green, *Illustrations for Biblical Preaching,* 398, quoted in Petro, *Discover Your Gift of Fragrance,* 100. Reprinted with permission.

23. Henry Gariepy, *Portraits of Christ* (Grand Rapids, Mich.: Revell, 1974), quoted in Kirkie Morrissey, *In His Name* (Colorado Springs, Colo.: NavPress, 1984), 83.

About the Authors

Sandra P. Aldrich is president and CEO of Bold Words, Inc., based in Colorado Springs. She is a the former senior editor of *Focus on the Family* magazine. She is the author of more than five hundred published magazine articles and seven books, and she is coauthor of or contributor to twenty more. She is a frequent speaker at women's and couples' retreats, military bases, grief workshops, college chapels, and parenting seminars. Sandra holds a master's degree from Eastern Michigan University and is the widowed mother of two adult children.

Bobbie Valentine is the president and CEO of Bobbie Valentine Media Consulting, Inc. She was formerly the executive producer of the Focus on the Family daily radio broadcast, where she worked closely with Dr. James Dobson for more than seventeen years. Before joining Focus, she taught for ten years at Biola University, where she developed a theater program. Bobbie holds a master's degree from the University of Michigan and is the widowed mother of two grown children, foster mother of one, and grandmother of seven.